IMAGES
of America

LUBBOCK

City of Lubbock Annexation History by Decade

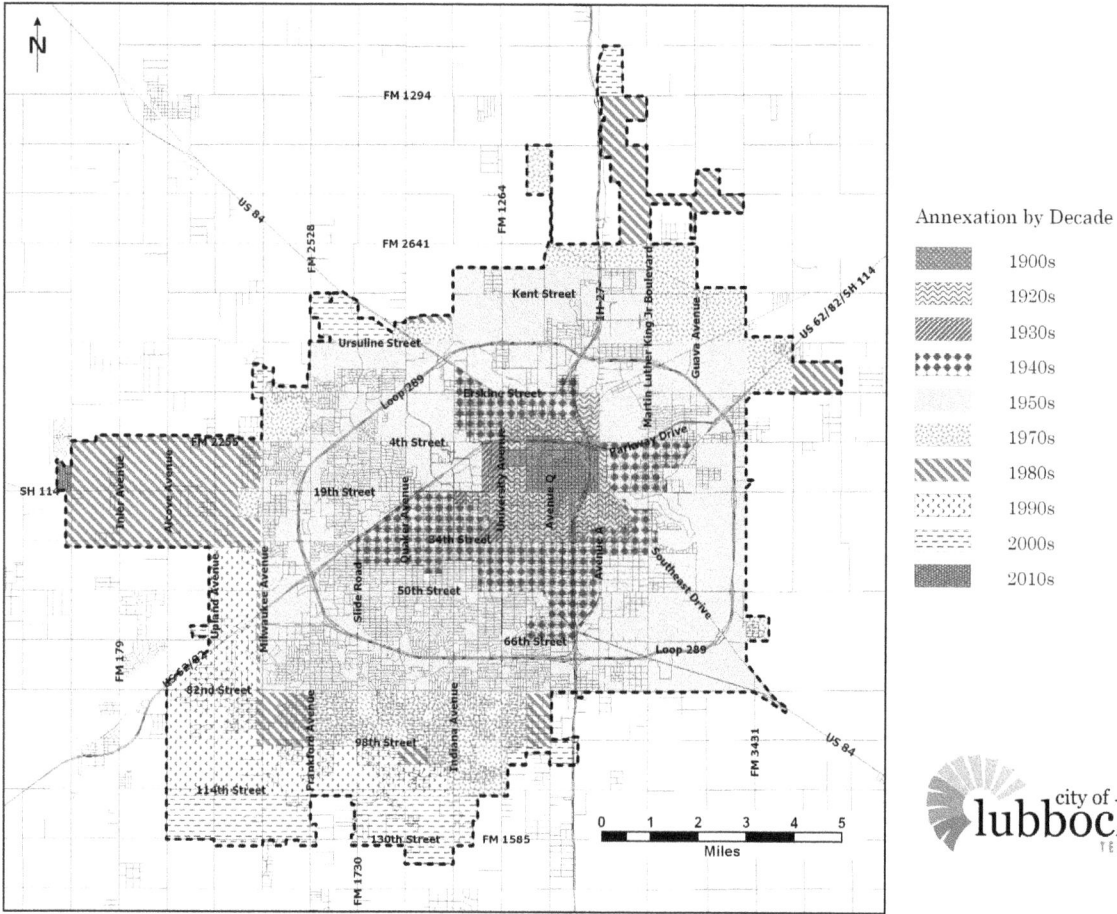

Annexation by Decade

- 1900s
- 1920s
- 1930s
- 1940s
- 1950s
- 1970s
- 1980s
- 1990s
- 2000s
- 2010s

city of
lubbock
TEX

City of Lubbock annexation history is shown by decades. From its beginnings in 1890 through 1960, Lubbock virtually doubled its population each decade, continually annexing new lands to accommodate population growth. With a population of 233,740 in 2011, Lubbock stands as the largest US city on the drier western side of the Great Plains. (Courtesy of City of Lubbock.)

On the Cover: Participants wend their way down Broadway in the American Business Club (ABC) Rodeo Parade around 1947, joining in a time-honored Lubbock tradition of organizing and gathering for a parade on Broadway, the street that serves as the historic artery of the town. (Courtesy of Southwest Collection.)

IMAGES
of America

LUBBOCK

Lubbock Heritage Society
Pamela Brink, Cindy Martin, and Daniel Sánchez

ARCADIA
PUBLISHING

Published by Arcadia Publishing
Charleston, South Carolina

Library of Congress Control Number: 2013949989

For all general information, please contact Arcadia Publishing:
Telephone 843-853-2070
Fax 843-853-0044
E-mail sales@arcadiapublishing.com
For customer service and orders:
Toll-Free 1-888-313-2665

Visit us on the Internet at www.arcadiapublishing.com

We dedicate this book to all the Lubbock people
who help keep our past a living part of the present by honoring
our heritage and saving and sharing their photographs, their
memorabilia, and their stories of this ever-growing and changing
town. Because of their farsightedness, generations to come will know
more and know better as they face the challenges of the future.

Contents

ACKNOWLEDGMENTS

The authors want to thank the Texas Tech University Southwest Collection/Special Collections Library for sharing its rich archive of historic photographs with us. We also want to thank the Lubbock Heritage Society for sponsoring this effort, and the willing participants in the Lubbock Heritage Society Photo Roundups organized to discover new historic photographs for this publication. To the many other individuals and organizations that so generously contributed images for this project, we are very grateful. Finally, we want to thank the professional scholars who have assiduously studied the history of Lubbock. Without their diligence, we would have been left with little context for many of the images that comprise this book

We express our deep appreciation to Dr. Lawrence L. Graves for editing a three-volume collection of articles published by the West Texas Museum Association entitled *The History of Lubbock* and another edited volume entitled *Lubbock: From Town to Gown*. For an in-depth perspective on the challenges and achievements of Texas Tech, we have found the following two volumes both informative and inspirational: Ruth Horn Andrews's *The First Thirty Years: A History of Texas Technological College, 1925–1955* and Jane Gilmore Rushing and Kline A. Nall's book *Evolution of a University: Texas Tech's First Fifty Years*. We are also grateful to Nancy Brooker Bronwell for her book *Lubbock: A Pictorial History*. Supported by the Lubbock Heritage Society, in 1989, Drs. Donald Abbe, Paul H. Carlson, and David J. Murrah published a history of the region entitled *Lubbock and the South Plains: An Illustrated History*. This work remains especially illuminating for understanding the agricultural dynamics of Lubbock and the towns that comprise its large trade region. Dr. Paul H. Carlson has written the most current and comprehensive study of the city entitled *The Centennial History of Lubbock: Hub City of the Plains*, published in 2008 as part of Lubbock's 100th birthday celebration. We offer a very special thank-you to Dr. Carlson for his seminal history and his willingness to assess our efforts by editing the manuscript for this visual journey through Lubbock.

INTRODUCTION

With a current population of 233,740, Lubbock, Texas, is the largest city on the drier, western side of the Great Plains, about 400 miles away from any larger place no matter what direction. Perched 3,000 feet up on a mesa, 300 miles across and up and down, Lubbock rises out of a seemingly endless flatland as a vital service center for the smaller communities of West Texas and eastern New Mexico. Surrounded by cotton fields, occasional prairie, and a vast unencumbered sky, Lubbock exists in urban isolation, relying primarily upon its own energetic resourcefulness to thrive and grow.

It has been this way since first settlement, when people living in two small hamlets near an ancient water site picked up their belongings and moved to a new location, joining their numbers to claim the county seat. Before the railroad came to town, they had already turned the old Army trails leading to that nearby water site into traversable roads and started buying and selling the abundant and fertile acreage all around them to swell the population. They spent years stumping for a railroad and, in 1909, it finally arrived, turning a primitive and newly incorporated town of 1,900 people into an established marketplace, with stone buildings, concrete sidewalks, and brick streets. They had also experimented with the crop capabilities of this virgin land and discovered a strain of cotton that would produce abundant harvests, leading to the development of a cotton supply and distribution industry for the town.

With the promise of a consistent cash crop in place, business growth supporting increased production, and three stable banks nurturing Lubbock's commercial enterprise, town leaders set their sights on gaining a state-funded college, once again stumping for Lubbock, this time through a barrage of newspaper editorials, coalitions with neighboring towns, and strong representation in Austin. Their efforts paid off, and in 1923, Lubbock was chosen as the site for a new college to serve all the people of West Texas. Combined with the railroad, and soon a paved highway system with Lubbock as the spoke, Texas Technological College gave the town a new pathway for consistent growth. Even during the hard, parched years of the 1930s, Lubbock remained stable and resourceful, taking full advantage of New Deal programs to put people to work and improving the infrastructure of the town.

Through most of its history, Lubbock has been fortunate to elect capable politicians. US Congressman George H. Mahon went to Washington in 1934 and served Texas District 19 until 1978. In World War II, he secured two Army bases for Lubbock, bringing soldiers and support personnel from all over the nation to town. When the war ended, Mahon made sure Lubbock kept the training program, creating Reese Air Force Base.

By 1950, Lubbock had a population of 71,745, with agribusiness, Texas Technological College, and Reese Air Force Base serving as its economic anchors. The GI Bill brought returning soldiers to Texas Tech, swelling the student population to 7,229 by 1955. As lieutenant governor, then governor of Texas, longtime Lubbock representative Preston E. Smith brought his influence to bear on supporting Lubbock. He helped make sure Texas Tech became part of the state university system and established the Texas Tech Law School and Medical School.

For its first 50 years, Lubbock virtually doubled its population every decade, and by 1960 that population included growing Hispanic and African American communities. Over the years, these two communities grew in stability within the confines of their own neighborhoods but soon found a voice in the decision-making centers of the town. While the F5 tornado that ravaged downtown Lubbock in 1970 changed the social and cultural configuration of the town, it did not change the spirit of resourcefulness that has always characterized the community. Lubbock rebuilt its downtown and neighborhoods with a new, more inclusive public vision.

As a self-contained urban center, Lubbock has nurtured its own way of doing things. Economically, it has always been energetically responsive to new enterprise, both commercial and educational. Culturally, it has always been slow to change. The longtime hegemony of this churchgoing town built a social lifestyle rooted in religious practice. Today, the city has over 200 churches of every conceivable denomination, including a Jewish temple and Islamic center, and people continue a long tradition of weekly worship. They also continue a long tradition of ecumenical cooperation in providing vital social services to the community.

The remoteness of Lubbock has nurtured a distinctive brand of music-making that has shaped popular styles since people began to listen to the radio. From the instrumental talents of early fiddle players to the dance music of the 1950s, to songwriters, singers, and instrumentalists in the ensuing decades, Lubbock continues to provide the nation with an inordinate number of gifted entertainers who send their music out into the world with important lessons learned from being a part of this isolated urban place.

Today, Lubbock is still growing with an energy and sense of pride that breathes confidence into virtually every new endeavor. The challenges of the 21st century will require new assessments of many tried-and-true ways, including water, land, and city resources, but if the leadership and community spirit of the first 100 years can serve as an example, Lubbock will greet the future with an industry and ingenuity that ensures it will thrive and grow for centuries to come.

One

SETTLING DOWN

Lubbock, Texas, became a townsite in December 1890. After the last bands of Plains Indians were confined to the Oklahoma Territory and the buffalo hunters had virtually eliminated the southern herd, the vast plateau called the Llano Estacado was organized for settlement. Investors soon began to purchase public lands available in the newly created counties. By 1889, two small towns had been established very near each other on the edge of an ancient water source that Spanish traders called La Punta de Agua. The promoters of these two communities soon realized they should merge at a new townsite and share the population benefits of securing the Lubbock County seat. Within a month, inhabitants of both towns moved their dwellings to present downtown Lubbock. Within a year, they had built a courthouse and a thriving business community.

The practical spirit of cooperation that created Lubbock remained a characteristic of town leadership throughout the early years of the city, with townspeople consistently acting as a unified force to support the community. Religious denominations shared services in the early years, and then helped each other raise the funds to build their churches. Town leaders joined together to build a cotton gin and worked tirelessly to bring a railroad through the town.

Lubbock was incorporated in 1909, with a population of almost 1,900. That same year, the Santa Fe Railway arrived and the town graduated its first high school class. Lubbock was a frontier town in a 20th-century world, with telephone service, electricity, motion pictures, and 100 automobiles before it had a water and sewage system, law enforcement, or reliable city streets. A municipal government changed all that. The next challenge was a college. Town leaders received support from Sen. William A. Bledsoe and banded together to secure the required 1,800 acres of land to assure legislators Lubbock was the right place for Texas Technological College. They were persuasive. On August 23, 1923, Lubbock became the home of an independent, coeducational college authorized to serve all of West Texas.

This is the escarpment of the Llano Estacado, a plateau over 3,000 feet up and 300 miles long and wide. Lubbock is located at an ancient water source on the southern edge of this vast grassland. Nomadic peoples and Spanish traders traversed the region and relied upon this rare source of water for centuries before anyone ever thought of settling down. The buffalo hunters were the

A windblown family is shown at the Estacado home of Dr. William Hunt in 1881. Paris Cox established the Quaker colony of Estacado in 1879. Located on the eastern edge of Lubbock County, Estacado was the first permanent settlement in the region. George Singer arrived at the colony in 1882, and then left in 1884 to establish a store at La Punta de Agua. (Courtesy of Southwest Collection.)

last to range the area and use the ancient lake site as a seasonal oasis. By 1880, they had virtually eliminated the southern herd, and speculators arrived to stake claims on unallocated lands in the Texas public domain. The lush grasses soon brought sheepherders to the area, followed by cattle ranchers. (Courtesy of Southwest Collection.)

Rollie Burns runs cattle at his Idlewild Ranch near newly established Lubbock. Burns came to the area as ranch manager of the IOA Ranch, established in 1884 and comprising virtually half of Lubbock County south of present-day Nineteenth Street. Frank Wheelock was general manager. When the IOA was sold off in 1901, Wheelock and Burns were already involved in building the town of Lubbock. (Courtesy of Southwest Collection.)

The three-story, 18-room Nicolett Hotel was the most imposing structure in the region in the 1890s. The Nicolett has always served as a symbol of the spirit of cooperation that merged two budding communities to establish Lubbock. All structures from the two communities were moved to the new townsite, with the Nicolett relocated to Courthouse Square, proudly reflecting the grand aspirations of this new prairie community. (Courtesy of Southwest Collection.)

At an 1899 Fourth of July barbecue, the whole Lubbock population of around 300 seems to be attending the festivities, beneath a rare grove of trees. For the most part, people devised their own fun—visiting at the barbershop or courthouse, holding picnics and barbecues, or going on fishing and hunting trips—but Fourth of July celebrations were large, organized, jubilant public gatherings. (Courtesy of Southwest Collection.)

The J.D. Caldwell store was located on the west side of Courthouse Square. Caldwell sold farm and ranch supplies and hauled the materials in by mule-drawn wagons from the railheads in Amarillo and Colorado City. (Courtesy of Southwest Collection.)

Located on Seventeenth Street and Avenue K, this was the home of Mr. and Mrs. Elder Penney in 1900. Downtown Lubbock is visible to the north. The family made their home as self-sufficient as possible, with a garden, fruit trees, windmill, a milk cow, horse, and water for their livestock. (Courtesy of Southwest Collection.)

An early Lubbock livery stable and wagon yard was located just behind the Nicolett Hotel, with a stately Eclipse windmill as part of the view. The signage in the photograph indicates the operation was a wagon yard, but the buggies on display suggest this business also provided animal-drawn vehicles for hire as a livery stable. (Courtesy of Southwest Collection.)

The Murphy Lumber Company and busy office next door illustrate the complications of building a town without a railroad. Like Caldwell's, this company relied upon mule-drawn wagon trains to bring all construction materials from Amarillo, Colorado City, and sometimes as far away as Fort Worth, a journey that could take more than a month. (Courtesy of Southwest Collection.)

14

The first Lubbock courthouse was built in 1891. The courthouse was the center of social and official activities. Religious denominations took turns with services every week and the literary club met there. Ballroom dancing was prohibited, but with an organ on the second floor, people enjoyed square dancing. In 1895, a mighty sandstorm blew off the original central tower of the courthouse, never to be replaced. (Courtesy of Southwest Collection.)

Settlers gather on a busy downtown street in early Lubbock. By 1907, business owners had established the Commercial Club as a booster organization. The growing commercial community could see far beyond the clapboard structures, dusty unpaved streets, and intermittent wooden sidewalks to the promise of this new century. (Courtesy of Southwest Collection.)

15

This flyer shows the first Lubbock schoolhouse, a three-room structure located on Fifteenth Street and Avenue I (Texas Avenue). The building burned down in 1909, and the 493 students enrolled that fall met in temporary quarters until a new brick building was completed. Education had changed significantly since 1891 when Minnie Tubbs offered subscription schooling at the county jail to 25 students who attended intermittently. (Courtesy of Southwest Collection.)

Lubbock Public School Announcement.

The Lubbock Public School will open Monday morning, September 4th. It is the earnest desire of the teachers that the patrons and others interested in school work be present. The opening exercises will be short and we believe the time spent in that way, true especially of the patrons, will be well invested. So come out and be with us and thus lend encouragement to your children, also to the teachers and promote school interest in general.

Following is a short program which will be rendered:

Song—by School.
Invocation—Rev. Walter Griffith.
Talk—by Judge Bean.
Recitation—Miss Mabel Penney.
Instrumental Music.
Talk—by Rev. B. F. Dixon.
Recitation—Miss Fannie Young.
Talk—to be supplied.
Instrumental Music.
Recitation—Miss Ruby McPherson.
Song.
Remarks by E. C. Finch.

This program is rather informal so anyone present who has a word of encouragement will feel at perfect liberty to speak.

All pupils should have their report cards ready to present to the teacher in charge.

Respectfully,
E. C. Finch, Principal.

This is the home of the weekly *Lubbock Avalanche* around 1900. The *Leader* was the first town newspaper, established by an Estacado attorney in 1891. It lasted until 1899. A year later, J.J. Dillard and Thad Tubbs created the *Lubbock Avalanche*, first distributed as a surprise, "like an 'avalanche' hits," Dillard explained. Early editors Dillard and James Dow were tireless promoters of Lubbock. In 1926, the paper became the *Lubbock Avalanche-Journal*. (Courtesy of Southwest Collection.)

This 1903 image shows the busy Dillard-Powell Land Company. In 1902, Texas ranch leases expired, and an abundance of land became available for settlement. Farmers were able to secure 640 acres of Texas school land at $2 per acre and three more sections for $1 per acre with 40 years to pay at five percent interest. Land-hungry settlers swept into Lubbock County. (Courtesy of Southwest Collection.)

Rev. Ben F. Dixon and his daughters are at the Baptist church in 1908. Built in 1901, the Baptist church was the first religious structure in Lubbock, followed by the Methodist church in 1905 and the Church of Christ in 1907. Lubbock settlers were devoted Protestants who originally shared religious observances and then helped each other finance their church structures. (Courtesy of Southwest Collection.)

To accommodate expanding cotton production, community leaders joined forces to build Lubbock's first cotton gin, shown here with cotton bales lined up for processing. Frank Wheelock supervised construction, and the gin was opened in time for the 1905 harvest. Lubbock was now poised to become a regional cotton agribusiness center. (Courtesy of Southwest Collection.)

Wagons loaded with cotton sit at the courthouse in 1906. A story goes that when one of the first Lubbock cotton crops was hauled to the nearest gin 150 miles away in Colorado City, the farmer was called a liar and arrested for robbery, because no one believed cotton would grow on the South Plains. By 1906, the evidence was in. Cotton would definitely grow up here. (Courtesy of Southwest Collection.)

Established in 1906,
Citizens National Bank
was guided by the business
acumen of George C.
Wolfforth in the early
years. Wolfforth owned a
ranch where the Lubbock
Country Club now
stands. Sam C. Arnett
soon became president
of Citizens National and
led it to prominence
as one of Lubbock's
longtime leading financial
institutions. (Courtesy of
Southwest Collection.)

In 1910, a US Post Office buggy leaves the Nicolett Hotel with a tag-along passenger for mail delivery to Plainview. By 1912, the Lubbock-to-Plainview circuit would make mail deliveries by automobile. (Courtesy of Southwest Collection.)

Pictured in 1914, the C.E. Hunt Grocery Store was located next to Frank Wheelock's real estate company on Courthouse Square. The Hunts were originally part of the Estacado Quaker community, and then moved to Lubbock. George M. Hunt was C.E.'s grandfather and was the first manager of the Nicolett Hotel. C.E. later became administrator at the Lubbock Sanitarium. (Courtesy of Southwest Collection.)

St. Paul's on the Plains, Lubbock's first Episcopal church, was built in 1913. The church was originally located at Fifteenth and Avenue O. In 1996, the Lubbock Heritage Society sponsored the relocation and restoration of the church at the Lubbock Arboretum. St. Paul's is the oldest existing church building in Lubbock and is now available to the general public as an events venue. (Courtesy of Cindy Martin.)

20

The 1906 Lubbock Band poses for an official Fourth of July photograph. From the beginning, the townspeople appreciated instrumental music and persisted in organizing band after band to play at public celebrations. Ross Edwards came to town in 1907; when people discovered he was a fiddler, they immediately organized a dance. Edwards's talents brought him recognition and influence. He became mayor of Lubbock in 1934. (Courtesy of Southwest Collection.)

Lubbock had automobiles, telephone service, and electricity before it had water and sewage systems, concrete sidewalks, or paved streets. While the primitive roads made driving challenging, by 1909, when this photograph was taken, Lubbock had at least three car agencies and over 100 automobiles in the county. (Courtesy of Southwest Collection.)

Lubbock is pictured around 1910 in this view looking south from Fourth Street. The two seeming rivulets are Avenue J and Texas Avenue. Bowered by the trees of Courthouse Square, the original wooden courthouse and crenellated brick county jail are visible to the distant left. With a population of almost 1,900, Lubbock voted to incorporate on March 6, 1909, bringing needed improvements to the living conditions of the town. (Courtesy of William Winner.)

The Santa Fe passenger train enters Lubbock for the first time on October 25, 1909. For a decade, the Commercial Club and other boosters had been trying to entice a railroad company to come to town. Finally, the Santa Fe chose Lubbock all on its own. When the first train arrived, the whole town turned out to celebrate this life-changing event. (Courtesy of Southwest Collection.)

The Lubbock Santa Fe Depot was built in 1911. Soon, the Santa Fe ran two rail lines through Lubbock. Reaching the town in 1911, the "Coleman cutoff" gave people access to transcontinental railroad service and a place on the Santa Fe main line. (Courtesy of Southwest Collection.)

Broadway is obstructed by a small playa after a torrential rain around 1912. To the right, Lubbock State Bank is decked out with a new stone facade. Incorporation quickly established the basic amenities of town life, like water mains, sewage lines, firefighters, police, and control of prowling cows and dogs on Courthouse Square. Reliable streets, however, were still a ways away. (Courtesy of Southwest Collection.)

Security State Bank and Trust and the Merrill Hotel face south at Texas Avenue and Main Street in 1917. Chartered in that year, Security State Bank joined Citizens National Bank and Lubbock State Bank in ensuring a stable financial foundation for the town. Security State Bank and Trust soon became Lubbock National Bank, and Lubbock State Bank was rechartered as First National Bank in 1921. (Courtesy of Ken Sharpe.)

Crowds gather at a Lubbock Trade Days event in 1913. Lubbock businesses were always promoting the town as a regional trade center, and the chamber of commerce was soon advertising Lubbock as "The Hub of the Plains." Trade Days were held monthly or seasonally, with special sales and the atmosphere of a county fair. People came from miles around in more numbers than the town could comfortably accommodate. (Courtesy of Southwest Collection.)

This is the 1916 Lubbock High School football team. In 1915, R.B. Gilbraith became the first paid coach in the Lubbock school system. Baseball was the most popular sport at the time, and Gilbraith led his team to wins over regional colleges. He also developed a football team. By 1917, the Westerners were unbeaten. College football would soon capture the hearts of the townspeople completely. (Courtesy of Southwest Collection.)

A 1915 festooned parade car is on its way past the courthouse and county jail. Parades celebrated the wholesome spirit of the town. In 1891, Lubbock shut down the only saloon; in 1910, both town and county banned liquor sales; and in 1914, the town banned pool halls. Prohibition had little effect on Lubbock. By 1919, bootlegging was already a time-honored, well-established local enterprise. (Courtesy of Cindy Martin.)

A street scene shows the Lyric Theater on the west side of Courthouse Square. Motion pictures played at the Opera House and the Orpheum Theater as early as 1909. By 1913, the Lyric Theater had opened and was well positioned to attract farm families in town for supplies. Matinees at 10¢ for adults and 5¢ for children were very popular with waiting farmwives and children. (Courtesy of Ken Sharpe.)

The first nursing class poses with the first ambulance at Lubbock Sanitarium on Broadway and Avenue L in 1918. The hospital opened just in time for the flu epidemic. Nurses training here and at West Texas Sanitarium were a vital component in making Lubbock a regional medical center. Ultimately owned by Drs. J.T. Hutchinson, J.T. Krueger, and M.C. Overton, Lubbock Sanitarium later became Methodist Hospital. (Courtesy of Southwest Collection.)

The second Lubbock County Courthouse was erected in 1915–1916. Built of stone, this three-story Neoclassical Revival structure gave an air of grandeur and elegance to the city. With a gazebo on the lawn, a stately brick county jail to the east, and thriving businesses surrounding the site, Courthouse Square continued to be the center of town with new stature and promise. (Courtesy of Ken Sharpe.)

This image shows the arduous work of laying the brick streets on Texas Avenue between the Courthouse and Lubbock National Bank. In 1920, Lubbock finally decided to float a bond issue and begin the process of paving the streets. The Panhandle Construction Company of Plainview received the first paving contract ever let by the city to brick 20 blocks of downtown Lubbock. (Courtesy of Southwest Collection.)

Milford Kittrell and a war buddy stand ready during their World War I tour overseas. While the war raged in Europe from 1914 to 1918, the United States avoided the conflict until 1917, when young men from all over the nation joined the fighting. World War I brought on national commodity shortages that led to soaring cotton prices and Lubbock boom times starting in 1918. (Courtesy of Don Kittrell.)

Thomas Martin and his dog, Fido, are standing in front of Martin's Shoe Shop in the 1920s. Martin's business was located in the 1200 block of Avenue H (Buddy Holly Avenue) and represents the casual commercial environment of downtown Lubbock. It was still a town of small, family-owned storefronts clustered around Courthouse Square. (Courtesy of Bobby T. Hughes.)

Cotton bales are ready for shipment in front of soon-to-be First National Bank of Lubbock. By 1920, the automobile had led to the development of a local industry of car dealerships, machine shops, and gas stations, but Lubbock was surrounded by agricultural enterprises still relying on livestock for work and transportation, revealing a stark contrast between Lubbock's modern ways and the old ways of the cotton industry nurturing its prosperity. (Courtesy of Southwest Collection.)

The Warren and Myrta Bacon House at 1802 Broadway was built in 1916. This elegant Neo-Classical home was one of the first built in the Overton Addition, an enterprise of first physician and city leader M.C. Overton that offered land for purchase just west of downtown. The Bacon House served as a signpost for further residential construction along Broadway in the coming decade. (Courtesy of Whit Rix Victory estate.)

The locating committee of the Texas legislature visits Lubbock as a possible site for a new college. On August 23, 1923, Lubbock was chosen for the school thanks to its central location, the influence of state senator William H. Bledsoe, and the foresight of city leaders who secured the required 1,800 acres for the site and promised street, water, and sewer extensions at Lubbock's expense. (Courtesy of Southwest Collection.)

A community picnic and jubilee was held on August 28, 1923, to celebrate Lubbock gaining Texas Technological College. The Lubbock Chamber of Commerce sponsored the grand event and invited all of West Texas. Around 30,000 people descended on the town, overflowing the streets, Courthouse Square, and downtown businesses to welcome a "first-class, coeducational, senior college" to the region. (Courtesy of Southwest Collection.)

Two

THE HUB OF THE PLAINS

The opening of Texas Technological College in 1925 gave Lubbock a promising new avenue for continued growth and prosperity. Broadway soon became a brick-paved boulevard from town to gown. New businesses sprang up to accommodate a growing number of students and visitors to Tech, and the Overton Addition quickly developed into a college neighborhood, full of student apartments, boardinghouses, and stately homes built for professors and deans.

By 1925, the cotton industry was solidly established as the cash crop of the South Plains. Lubbock took the lead as the agribusiness center, providing area cotton farmers with cottonseed oil mills, cotton gins, cotton compresses, irrigation equipment, well-drilling expertise, and other marketing resources to support the crop. The varied jobs associated with the growing cotton harvest brought African American and Hispanic workers to town. Each year, more and more stayed on to make Lubbock their permanent home.

The financial crisis and prolonged drought of the 1930s brought many hardships to the town, but the resourcefulness and unity of the business community helped Lubbock weather the economic and environmental storms of the era. The Lubbock Loyalty Council, organized through the chamber of commerce, helped protect the three local banks by convincing Lubbock citizens their money was secure. When the prolonged bank holiday was over in Texas, Lubbock stood out as a very rare town, with no bank closings. Instead, people lined up to make deposits.

Lubbock was also enterprising in securing a number of New Deal grants to put people to work while improving the city infrastructure. Through Works Progress Administration and Civilian Conservation Corps funding, Mackenzie Park was graced with a number of beautification projects, including a public swimming pool. WPA workers were also involved in curb and gutter projects and the accidental discovery of what would become a very important archeological site at La Punta de Agua.

In 1920, Lubbock had a population of 4,051. By 1940, Lubbock had a population of 31,853, with the promise of new opportunities for development through the important role the town would play during World War II.

The Texas Technological College Administration Building was completed in 1925. September 30 marked the official opening, when a faculty of 43 welcomed 914 students to a vast, underdeveloped campus. The Administration, Textile Engineering, and Home Economics buildings, along with the Stock Judging Pavilion and the Dairy Barn, were all there was for educational purposes until 1928–1929, when the Engineering and Chemistry buildings were finally completed. (Courtesy of Southwest Collection.)

This image shows the Texas Tech Dairy Barn in 1925. From 1926–1935, selected students were allowed to house three dairy cows and occupy spare rooms in the barn. The students tended their livestock and sold the milk. Prof. Kenneth M. Renner, head of the Department of Dairy Industry, managed the enterprise, helping students pay for their education and assisting the department in financing laboratory essentials. (Courtesy of Southwest Collection.)

The 1925 Matadors pose for their official team photograph. Dubbed "Red Raiders" under the coaching powers of Pete Cawthorn, Tech's football team was invited to the 1939 Cotton Bowl as undefeated champions of the Border Conference. Playing in a foot of mud, Tech lost to St. Mary's College. Team member Elmer Tarbox noticed the mud had made his legs stronger, leading him to patent Elmer's Weights exercise equipment. (Courtesy of William Winner.)

This is an early photograph of the Textile Engineering Building. Texas Technological College was established to serve the practical needs of West Texas, originally offering degrees in liberal arts, home economics, engineering, and agricultural sciences. The Textile Engineering Department helped nurture the regional cotton industry. The first Texas Tech president, Paul Whitfield Horn, was proud to wear a cotton suit and accessories woven and tailored by the department. (Courtesy of Southwest Collection.)

This 1920s aerial view of Lubbock looks west from Broadway and Texas Avenue. With Lubbock Sanitarium, First Methodist Church, and Lubbock High School in clear view, this photograph shows the extent of downtown commercial development in the decade following World War I. (Courtesy of Whit Rix Victory estate.)

The Young Men's Bible Class stands in front of the First Methodist Church in 1926. Texas Tech's first president, Paul W. Horn, became the teacher of this class. He is center stage in the front row, sporting his white $1 cotton suit, hand-loomed and tailored for him by the talents available in the Texas Tech Department of Textile Engineering. (Courtesy of Bob and Betty Carr.)

In this 1926 barbershop scene, a female customer has joined the men. In the 1920s, young Lubbock women followed the trend of sporting permanent waves and frequenting the traditional male sanctum of the barbershop for short haircuts. Inspired by a new spirit of freedom with the right to vote, women also wore their dresses short and loose. (Courtesy of Bobby T. Hughes.)

The Texas Tech Saxophone Band performs in the late 1920s. Responding to the spirit of the times, Texas Tech coeds donned flapper outfits and joined this college ragtime band, eager to entertain, playing the dance rhythms of the Jazz Age. (Courtesy of Southwest Collection.)

Hotel Lubbock, a six-floor structure before its final addition, opened in 1925 anticipating new Texas Tech visitors to the town. Located at Broadway and Avenue K, it stood as the tallest building and most sophisticated lodging in Lubbock. Later, Hotel Lubbock became the Pioneer Hotel. Today, the preserved and renovated building is Pioneer Condos, offering space for residential and commercial purposes. (Courtesy of Southwest Collection.)

The Dallas-based Jack Gardner Orchestra provides its hot jazz music for a night of revelry celebrating the opening of Hotel Lubbock. From settlement days, the people of the town took every opportunity to organize a night of dancing. By the 1920s, Lawrence Graves estimates there were over 70 dance clubs of every kind in Lubbock, including square dancing, round dancing, and ballroom dancing. (Courtesy of Southwest Collection.)

The Fort Worth and Denver Railroad Depot was built with the opening of a rail line in 1928, giving the town additional transportation resources for the growing wholesale markets, shoppers, and college visitors. Today, the charming Spanish-style depot is home to the Buddy Holly Center and serves as an anchor to the Depot Entertainment District. (Courtesy of Southwest Collection.)

Lubbock High School, built in 1931, echoes the Spanish Renaissance style of the Texas Tech campus. The structure still stands today as the premier architectural jewel of the city. Facing Nineteenth Street in South Overton, Lubbock High is surrounded by a neighborhood developed in response to the opening of Texas Tech. Many houses have backyard, stand-alone apartments built for student housing. (Courtesy of Southwest Collection.)

Lubbock golfers play at Mackenzie Park during the national golf craze of the 1920s. In 1921, avid players organized the Lubbock Country Club, located on Wolfforth family farmland near the original site of the Nicolett Hotel and La Punta de Agua. In 1923, local sports promoter Sled Allen helped organize the public golf course at Mackenzie Park. It exists today as the Meadowbrook Golf Course. (Courtesy of Southwest Collection.)

A 1929 aerial view of the Panhandle South Plains Fair shows the latest models of tractors prominently on display. Organized in 1913, the Lubbock Chamber of Commerce helped make Lubbock the commercial center of the region. In 1924, A.B. Davis became the manager of the chamber and, in 1926, established the Panhandle South Plains Fair. Today, the fair boasts attendance of over 400,000 during the nine-day event. (Courtesy of Southwest Collection.)

This is a 1920s view of Broadway west of Avenue Q, with the H.O. Waters house on the right. As Texas Tech grew, people began to build homes on west Broadway and businesses developed along the street to cater to students, who often thumbed a ride from drivers chugging down Broadway. (Courtesy of Whit Rix Victory estate.)

The Frick Restaurant was a very popular dining spot during the 1920s. This interior view of the restaurant, with tin ceiling, tile floors, casual counter area, and formal seating, shows the humble but accommodating style of small Lubbock eateries in this era. (Courtesy of Southwest Collection.)

Northside Grocery is pictured in 1921. Located at 612 Avenue H (Buddy Holly Avenue), the grocery was owned by James E. Watson, shown in the middle. The previous owner and his son flank Watson on either side. They stayed around to help him get started with the enterprise. (Courtesy of Southwest Collection.)

This is the 1920s office headquarters for the South Plains division of the Texas Utilities Company. The building included a 50-ton electric-driven ice plant as part of the expansion program of the company to keep pace with the rapid development of the South Plains. (Courtesy of Southwest Collection.)

The Downtown Bible Class, shown here on Sunday, April 28, 1929, met at the Lyric Theater. Even though by this time the churches had their own buildings, the very devout community of Lubbock still welcomed the opportunity to share Bible study with people of other denominations. (Courtesy of Linda Adkins.)

L.M. Read is out standing in his field near Lubbock, with his house visible on the horizon two miles away. This bird's-eye view supports songwriter Butch Hancock's observation that in West Texas "if you stand on a tuna fish can, you can see a hundred miles." With no trees or brush to clear, Read could quickly plow the land under and plant cotton. (Courtesy of Whit Rix Victory estate.)

Two young men stand in high cotton in the early 1920s. During the postwar cotton boom, farmers planted fencerow to fencerow—and sometimes up to the back porch—in cotton. As the regional agribusiness center, Lubbock supported the industry with cotton gins, cottonseed oil mills, implement dealerships, seed companies, and other production resources. (Courtesy of Southwest Collection.)

This dapper young man proudly displays the car he drives. The first African Americans settled in Lubbock around 1916, building a residential and business community in the beautiful canyon area of town. Lubbock was rigidly segregated, with a residential line drawn at Avenue C north of Sixteenth Street. Within those confines, the Eastside grew and prospered as a church-based, neighborhood-centered community. (Courtesy of Southwest Collection.)

Five-year-old Rodney Goebel confidently drives a team of horses on the family farm in 1927. Before mechanization became almost universal in the late 1940s, farming remained a labor-intensive business on the South Plains. Children became a part of the family work crew at a very early age to help with the many challenging chores required to make ends meet, and maybe even prosper, through farming. (Courtesy of Rodney Goebel.)

Citizens National Bank was at Broadway and Texas Avenue in the 1930s. By 1932, the 1929 crash had turned into a national banking crisis. Citizens National, Lubbock National, and First National worked with the Lubbock Loyalty Council to reassure the community that Lubbock banks were solvent. When the doors opened after the bank holiday of March 1933, no Lubbock bank closed. People lined up to make deposits. (Courtesy of Whit Rix Victory estate.)

A dust storm as black as night surrounds a lone car on a Lubbock road in the so-called Dirty Thirties. The drought of 1930–1936 exacerbated the financial crisis. While Lubbock was south of the official dust bowl, it is always marked by seasonal high winds with accompanying sand in the air, and the town struggled environmentally, financially, and psychologically through these parched years. (Courtesy of Library of Congress.)

McIlhaney's horse-drawn milk delivery wagon is a charming example of the growth of the dairy industry in Lubbock during the late 1920s, when crop prices began falling years before the Wall Street crash. Dairy herds and the "cream check" became lifesavers to farmers. By 1930, Lubbock produced a fourth of the butter manufactured in Texas, and area farmers profited from a growing demand for ice cream. (Courtesy of Southwest Collection.)

Men lined up eager for a job as part of the emergency employment cleanup crew. In 1930, the newspaper reported a "shack town" in Lubbock and the death of three children. By 1932, over 25 percent of the American people were jobless. Lubbock County made efforts to respond to the crisis by providing emergency charity services and establishing a vegetable patch at Courthouse Square. (Courtesy of Southwest Collection.)

Texas Tech campus visitors are making the long trek from the Textile Engineering Building to the Administration Building. This view helps to explain why the students called Textile Engineering the "Amarillo Campus." While the Depression brought drastic cuts to faculty salaries and college operations, Tech gained student work opportunities, a campus sidewalk system, and landscaping services through New Deal relief programs. (Courtesy of Southwest Collection.)

West Hall was the first men's dormitory on the Texas Tech campus. In 1934, Tech received a WPA grant to build the first campus dormitories, one for men and one for women. From 1925 to 1934, virtually all students stayed in off-campus dormitories or boardinghouses, or rented small, stand-alone apartments built behind homes in the Overton neighborhood. (Courtesy of Southwest Collection.)

The wading pool at Mackenzie Park was built with New Deal funding. Through WPA and CCC grants, Lubbock was able to beautify Mackenzie Park with bridges, tree plantings, and other landscaping projects. In honor of the original prairie dog town spanning from Abilene to Amarillo, K.N. Clapp made a place for the prairie dog in what became Mackenzie State Park in 1935. (Courtesy of Southwest Collection.)

A new Lubbock County Jail was built in 1931. In 1920, the Lubbock population was 4,051; in 1930, it was 20,520. Designed in the contemporary Art Deco style, this building was in use as a jail until 2010. As one of the few Art Deco structures still standing in Lubbock, the building is on the Lubbock Heritage Society's endangered list. (Courtesy of Southwest Collection.)

The Lubbock County Post Office and Federal Building was built in 1932 through the successful efforts of A.B. Davis to establish federal offices in Lubbock. Besides the post office, the building housed the US District Court, IRS, Immigration Services, Army Recruitment, the Department of Agriculture, and New Deal Agencies. Today, the building is on the Texas list of top 10 endangered structures. (Courtesy of Southwest Collection.)

In 1928, the 12-story Lubbock Hilton Hotel opened, located at Main Street and Texas Avenue. The Hilton supplanted Hotel Lubbock as the tallest building in town. Sam Ribble had his florist shop at street level of the Hilton from 1931 to 1950. (Courtesy of the Ribble family.)

A view of the Hilton Hotel lobby shows tile, carvings, and other appointments fashioned after the popular Southwest style of La Fonda in Santa Fe. The Hilton brought a new sense of glamour and refinement to Lubbock. Known as the Caprock Hotel after 1955, the hotel was demolished in the 1960s to put in a drive-through banking facility. (Courtesy of Southwest Collection.)

In 1922, Hemphill-Wells opened its doors at Thirteenth Street and Avenue J as a premier Lubbock department store. Known for its quality merchandise and personal service, the store offered customers everything from a toaster to a fur coat and a nice meal in between. Hemphill-Wells was a cherished institution for generations of shoppers throughout the South Plains. (Courtesy of Southwest Collection.)

A McDonald Packing Company delivery truck in the 1930s sports contemporary advertising on the exterior. Along with many other family-owned Lubbock companies, McDonald's carved out a regional territory, delivering company products to homes and businesses throughout the extensive Lubbock trade area. (Courtesy of William Winner.)

The Spotted Pig Bar-B-Q was located at 3207 Avenue H (I-27 Access Road). With its Mission-style appointments, waitresses in snappy matching outfits, and a willow loveseat at the entrance, this sandwich place looks just about as welcoming as can be. (Courtesy of Southwest Collection.)

The W.C. Boyd Company filling station stands ready for business. By the 1930s, automobiles were a beloved part of everyday life. This service station was open 24-7, offering a car wash, machine shop, and an attendant at the pump. Some are still around who can tell the story of the full-service filling station. (Courtesy of Southwest Collection.)

The Nicolett Hotel looks a little worse for wear by 1935, but is at least still standing after all these years. Montgomery Ward is also visible in this Broadway street scene, an indication of the growing retail market in Lubbock. (Courtesy of Southwest Collection.)

The Kress Building was built at 1109 Broadway in 1932. Like Montgomery Ward, Kress was a national retail corporation, opening one of its five-and-dime stores in Lubbock. The distinctive Mission style of the building's facade has always served as a downtown touchstone. (Courtesy of Southwest Collection.)

Templo Hermosa musicians are shown in 1938. In 1920, the Lubbock School District built a school in the Guadalupe neighborhood, and in 1924, the Catholic Church built St. Joseph's, one of the oldest churches in Lubbock today. Many Hispanics came each fall to contribute to the cotton harvest. Each year, more and more decided to stay and become part of the community. (Courtesy of Southwest Collection.)

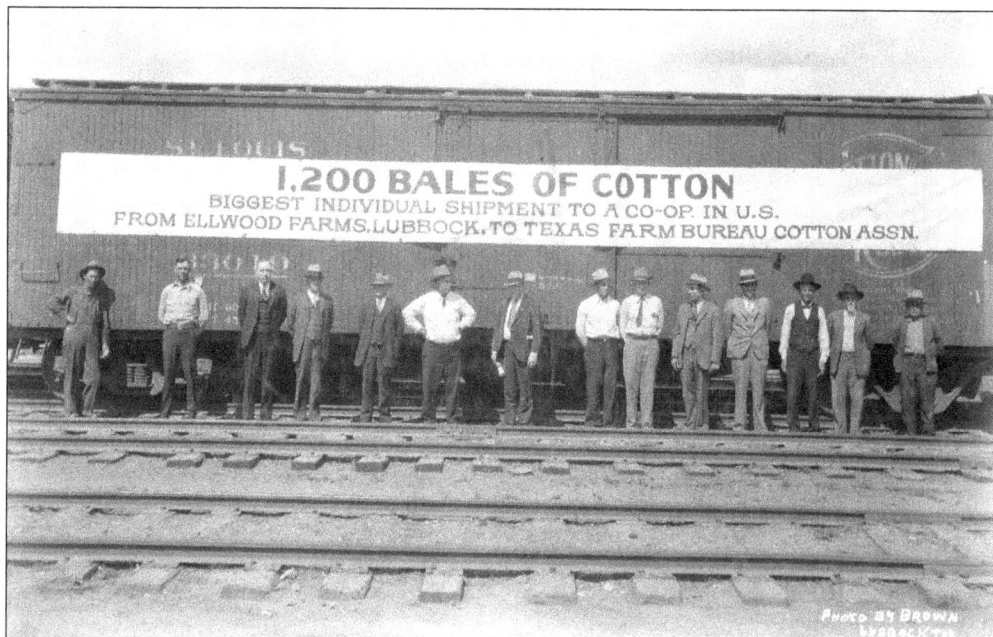

Ellwood Farms celebrates the 1930 cotton harvest. As the drought persisted over the years, more and more cotton farmers began to drill irrigation wells, finding the water supply from the Ogallala Aquifer plentiful and easy to access. Soon, Lubbock would be the center of the most mechanized farming region in the world. (Courtesy of Southwest Collection.)

The original 1938 Cotton Club was located at Fiftieth Street and the railroad tracks. The club was a very wet place in a very dry town where, Henry Lester insists, "The bootleggers had to wear name tags to keep from trying to sell to each other." The bootleggers were not alone. From December 1939 to April 1940, Lubbock physicians wrote out 168,745 prescriptions for liquor. (Courtesy of Sandy Fortenberry.)

The Drugstore Cowboys pose in front of radio station KFYO. Opening in 1932 as Lubbock's first radio station, KFYO gave talented musicians new opportunities to make a living. Fiddle player Henry Lester managed the Drugstore Cowboys, sponsored by Halsey Drugstore. Following Gov. Pappy O'Daniels's example, when Hop Halsey ran for state representative in 1934, he campaigned with and through the band. (Courtesy of Don and Sally Abbe.)

The Lubbock Hubbers play to an avid crowd. The Hubbers were a Lubbock semiprofessional baseball team, organized and reorganized in the town from 1922 to 1955. To help make their efforts more worthwhile, the Hubbers had a tradition of running the fences to collect tips from the fans after a particularly inspirational play. (Courtesy of Southwest Collection.)

A casual and curious crowd gathers at the first Lubbock Municipal Airport north of downtown. Established in 1933, the airport did not attract a commercial airline during the early years and was only used for private flying. However, it would soon become an important part of the national war effort. (Courtesy of Southwest Collection.)

Three

THE WINS OF WAR

Through the efforts of longtime congressman George H. Mahon, Lubbock became an important pilot-training site during World War II. Lubbock Army Air Field brought thousands of people through the town to become pilots and support the war effort. South Plains Army Air Field was also established in Lubbock and became the largest advance glider pilot training base in the world. The influx of people led to new residential development, retail enterprises, and transportation services that expanded the infrastructure of the town.

After the war, the Army retained the pilot training school, turning it over to Lubbock as Reese Air Force Base and creating a significant economic engine for the town over the next 50 years. Lubbock also profited from strong cotton prices after the war and an influx of students to Texas Technological College from returning soldiers taking advantage of the GI Bill.

In 1940, Lubbock had grown to a population of over 30,000, and by 1950 to over 70,000. The immediate postwar years brought every kind of construction to the town, from new retail stores to major church construction on Broadway and residential construction past Nineteenth Street.

By 1950, the Plaza Shopping Center was in full flower, leading the way to a new trend of building retail shops with convenient parking. The city was moving south, with Thirty-fourth Street developing into a major artery of vibrant mom-and-pop stores and drive-through hamburger joints.

The late 1940s saw a number of new and innovative radio stations established in Lubbock that served as important incubators for local musicians. Buddy Holly, Waylon Jennings, Sonny Curtis, and Bob Montgomery all got their starts as teenagers playing live spots for local radio stations.

Lubbockites tour the flight line on opening day of Lubbock Army Air Field. Established in June 1941 on city-donated acreage west of town, the airfield trained crews to fly advanced twin-engine planes, bringing to Lubbock a bustling military presence and thousands of new residents and commercial opportunities. Lubbock Army Air Field was one of 34 Army Air Force training sites during World War II. (Courtesy of Don and Sally Abbe.)

This jeep is being loaded on a glider at South Plains Army Air Field. In 1942, the US Army established a second base in Lubbock, located near the Lubbock Municipal Airport. It became the largest advance glider pilot–training base in the world. It also served as an ordnance depot. Through the efforts of Congressman George Mahon, four military bases were established in Texas District 19. (Courtesy of Don and Sally Abbe.)

A patriotic display graces a window of Lena Stephens Department Store. Lubbock had a deep commitment to the war effort and celebrated the pilots and aircrews training in Lubbock at every turn. (Courtesy of Southwest Collection.)

This photograph shows the 309th College Training Detachment at Texas Technological College. Through a campus military-training program, Texas Tech was able to counter a drastic drop in enrollment during the war. From 1943 to 1944, the program brought 4,747 military men to campus for course work in engineering, mathematics, science, history, English, physics, and other disciplines, accompanied by physical and military exercises. (Courtesy of Southwest Collection.)

Encouraging contributions to the scrap pile to help with metal shortages encountered during the war, an eager Boy Scout stands by a cartoon cutout of Hitler. Citizens were given the opportunity to "bring your pots and pan Hitler," with a bull's-eye on Hitler's behind helping inspire the toss. (Courtesy of Southwest Collection.)

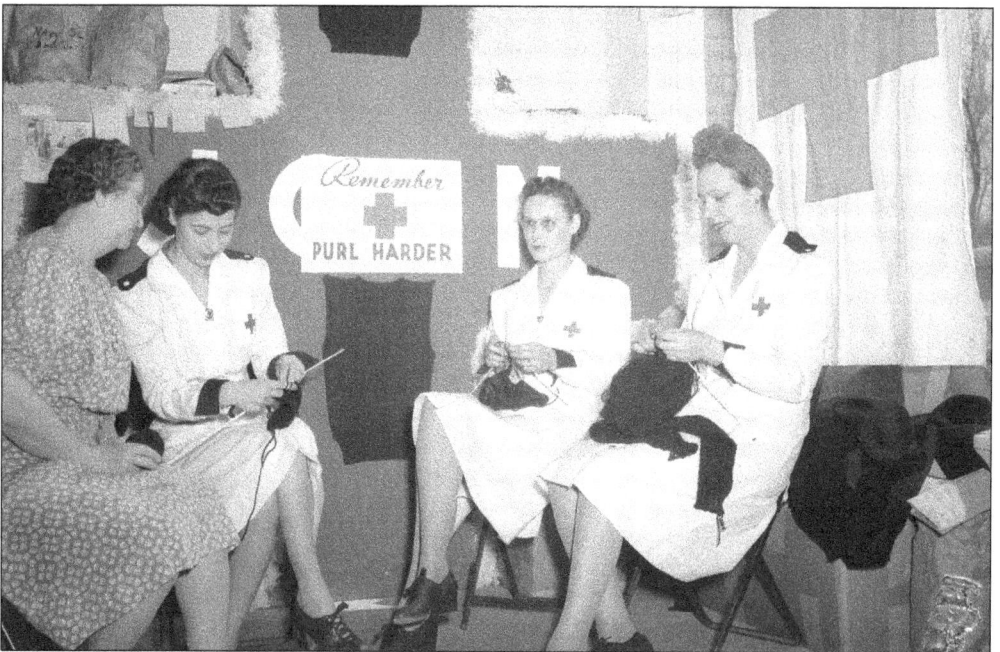

Red Cross volunteers knit for the war effort. They are inspired in their task by the motto "Remember Purl Harder." (Courtesy of Southwest Collection.)

Local young women entertain cadets at the Hilton Hotel ballroom in 1943. Lubbock citizens got involved in the USO in many ways to welcome all military personnel to town. (Courtesy of Southwest Collection.)

A local USO group welcomes black soldiers to Lubbock during their time in training. The military was still segregated during World War II. (Courtesy of Southwest Collection.)

Young women enjoy an afternoon in bustling downtown Lubbock. Shopping was a way to relax during the overseas combat struggles of 1942. (Courtesy of Southwest Collection.)

Green Acres Addition was constructed between Boston and Elgin from Twenty-fourth to Thirtieth Streets in 1941. The dramatic influx of people coming to Lubbock during the war caused a housing shortage. Green Acres and Hub Homes were built with federal funding to accommodate the demand, and when that was not enough, developers moved structures in from other towns and placed them near the bases. (Courtesy of Southwest Collection.)

A Lubbock resident crosses a downtown street in a rowboat after a torrential rain in 1941. A local saying goes, "If you don't like the weather in Lubbock, wait a minute." In 1941, if you waited a minute, it rained again. That year, the usual annual 18 inches of rainfall became a yearlong downpour of 40.55 inches, and people responded to the soaked conditions by sometimes using boats to get around. (Courtesy of Southwest Collection.)

A member of the Carpenter's Union pickets downtown, a very unusual sight in Lubbock. The Carpenter's Union was involved in a local labor dispute in the 1940s. (Courtesy of Southwest Collection.)

Chatman Hospital was built in 1945 to serve the black community of Lubbock and the South Plains. Located in Manhattan Heights, the hospital was established by Dr. J.A. Chatman, who was a noted physician and civic leader. In 1960–1961, Gov. Price Daniel appointed Dr. Chatman to the White House Conferences on aging and youth. (Courtesy of Southwest Collection.)

Dunbar High School 1945 seniors pose for a formal prom photo. At this time, blacks were still denied school bus transportation and excluded from Texas Technological College. The population continued to grow on the east side of town, and Dunbar was the heart of this community of over 2,000 in 1940. (Courtesy of Southwest Collection.)

King's Café, located at 2201 Date Avenue, was a popular eatery and gathering spot for the black community of Lubbock during the war years and beyond. (Courtesy of Southwest Collection.)

The Lubbock black community semiprofessional baseball team was also named the Hubbers. The team played other black baseball teams throughout the region off and on from the 1920s to 1956. That year, the team moved to wet Victoria, Texas, thinking that the availability of beer might encourage larger attendance at the games. (Courtesy of Southwest Collection.)

An avid weekend crowd gathers at the Lindsey Theater. Opening at 1019 Main Street in 1940, the Lindsey became one of the most popular places for weekend entertainment downtown. The movies were a welcome escape during the war, and Lubbock supported a number of movie theaters throughout the 1940s. (Courtesy of Southwest Collection.)

Santa visits the Llanos Theater at Fourth Street and Avenue G in the 1940s. The Llanos Theater was a favorite entertainment spot for the growing Hispanic community of Lubbock. The number of Hispanics in Lubbock swelled by thousands in the autumn, when seasonal workers came to town to help with the cotton harvest and spend their leisure hours downtown. (Courtesy of Southwest Collection.)

64

Mourners leave First Methodist Church on Broadway and Avenue M after the memorial service for Pres. Franklin Delano Roosevelt. The president died on April 12, 1945, and the country mourned. It was left to Pres. Harry S. Truman to end the prolonged hostilities and try to turn the nation back to long-neglected domestic concerns. (Courtesy of Southwest Collection.)

A returning soldier poses for a ceremonial photograph as he buys the first Ford sold in Lubbock after the war. The rationing was over and shortages were gradually coming to an end. People were eager to acquire goods long denied. (Courtesy of Southwest Collection.)

First Christian Church at Broadway and Avenue X was built in 1946. Even before the end of the war, the long-established churches were building on Broadway. By then, First Methodist and Broadway Church of Christ had already completed construction of new and imposing structures, and First Baptist soon followed. During the immediate postwar years, 26 Lubbock churches completed new additions and 38 churches completed new construction. (Courtesy of Southwest Collection.)

Margaret's was established on Broadway in 1947. Margaret's dress shop set the Lubbock standard in women's clothing for the next 40 years. Everyone wanted to be "A Margaret's Woman." Skibell's opened in downtown Lubbock in 1946, offering shoppers fine-quality men's and women's apparel. Malouf's quickly followed with sophisticated men's clothing, and Dunlap's opened a downtown department store, later moving its headquarters to Lubbock. (Courtesy of Southwest Collection.)

Lubbock passengers prepare to board the first Braniff Airways flight in 1945. Pioneer Airlines and Continental Airlines quickly followed with passenger services, as did Essair with freight services. Lubbock Municipal Airport was finally a growing transportation resource for the city. (Courtesy of Southwest Collection.)

The TNM&O bus station was built in 1947. During the war, TNM&O Bus Lines provided vital transportation services in Texas, New Mexico, and Oklahoma, bringing soldiers and military personnel to Lubbock and taking them to their next military destinations. With headquarters in Lubbock, the bus line continued to provide transportation services for decades. (Courtesy of Southwest Collection.)

Cars line the long esplanade to the developing engineering circle. By the 1940s, the Texas Tech campus was graced by trees and ongoing landscaping efforts. Desperately needed buildings would soon follow in growing abundance. (Courtesy of Rodney Goebel.)

This 1947 aerial view shows the Texas Tech campus bursting at the seams with new students. The college relied on leftover Army barracks to accommodate them. The GI Bill paid tuition and living expenses for returning soldiers, and they readily responded. Texas Tech enrollment was up from 2,443 in 1945 to 6,145 in 1948. It continued to rise radically throughout the 1950s. (Courtesy of Southwest Collection.)

The West Texas Museum was completed in 1950. Finally, funding became available to add a structure to the basement that had served as the repository for the museum's collection since 1938. In 1954, American artist Peter Hurd completed a 16-panel mural in the building rotunda celebrating the early pioneers of Lubbock. Today, the original museum is part of Holden Hall, named after museum founder Dr. Curry Holden. (Courtesy of Southwest Collection.)

Riding his horse, Blackie, Kirk Fulton leads the Texas Tech football team onto the field at the Gator Bowl in 1954. The Red Raiders won that game against the Auburn Tigers 35-13, and Fulton established a new and lasting Texas Tech tradition. Soon, a mask and the "guns up" sign were added to this dramatic persona named the Masked Rider. (Courtesy of Southwest Collection.)

Students eagerly rent bicycles from Dub Rushing's Varsity Bookstore to make their way around the Texas Tech campus and college business community in the 1940s. Located at 1305 University Avenue, Varsity Bookstore still serves the Texas Tech community today with textbooks, school supplies, and a wealth of Texas Tech sports memorabilia. (Courtesy of Southwest Collection.)

On Saturdays in the 1940s, downtown was packed with shoppers, gathering to visit as well as spend the weekly wages many had earned working the cotton harvest. Local merchants eagerly anticipated the annual autumn boost in sales. (Courtesy of Southwest Collection.)

Young men prepare to deliver the *Lubbock Evening Journal*, one of two daily editions of the *Lubbock Avalanche-Journal* in the 1940s. As editor of the paper from 1931 to 1972, Charles A. Guy wrote a very influential daily column called The Plainsman, establishing himself as a tireless promoter of Lubbock and the South Plains. (Courtesy of Southwest Collection.)

The League of United Latin American Citizens (LULAC) sponsors a famous Mexican film to benefit the organization. Out of a population of 71,747 in 1950, 669 residents were Hispanic. In 1951, the community established a chapter of LULAC. The chapter continues to serve the community today as an advocacy group and tireless promoter of Hispanic businesses. (Courtesy of Southwest Collection.)

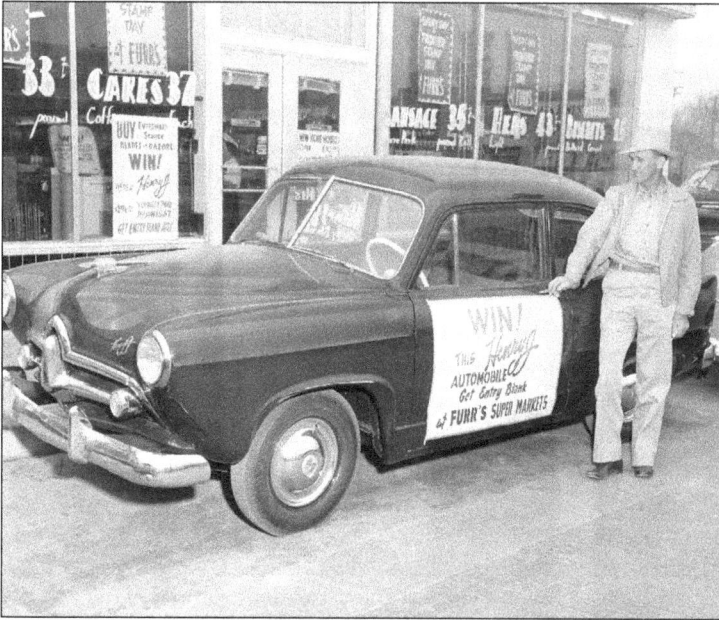

The new Furr's Super Market holds a drawing for a Henry J automobile, an inexpensive car built between 1950 and 1954 by Kaiser-Frazer Corporation. Established in Lubbock in 1929 and with division headquarters in Lubbock, Furr's grocery stores had expanded by 1950 to 26 stores in West Texas and New Mexico, including supermarkets and cafeterias. (Courtesy of Southwest Collection.)

The Lubbock Symphony Orchestra (LSO) performs at the Lubbock High School Auditorium in the 1950s. The orchestra presented its first concert in 1946 as an entirely volunteer organization under the baton of conductor William A. Harrod, who continued to lead the orchestra until 1984. The LSO became a professional organization with paid musicians in 1967 and continues today with a full annual calendar of exciting performances. (Courtesy of Southwest Collection.)

American State Bank was founded in 1948 with facilities at Fourteenth Street and Avenue Q. The growth of Lubbock was reflected in the growth of the banking industry. Long-established First National Bank, Lubbock National Bank, and Citizens National Bank experienced large increases in deposits and assets and constructed new buildings downtown. Established in 1953, Plains National Bank joined American State as another new financial institution. (Courtesy of Southwest Collection.)

Methodist Hospital was established in 1954 with the facilities to accommodate the needs of West Texas and eastern New Mexico. The hospital that began as Lubbock Sanitarium in 1917 became Lubbock General in 1941, Lubbock Memorial in 1945, and moved into a new 280-bed facility on Nineteenth Street in 1953. In 1954, Drs. Krueger, Overton, and Waggoner sold the hospital to the United Methodist Church to establish Methodist Hospital. (Courtesy of Covenant.)

Tommy Hancock's band The Roadside Playboys plays a dance around 1950. One of the most popular groups in Lubbock after World War II, the band was influenced by the western swing style of Bob Wills. Hancock played lead fiddle, and the band provided the Lubbock area dance crowd with the electric honky-tonk sounds that gave Texas dance music a distinctive place in the country music arena. (Courtesy of Southwest Collection.)

KSEL

WESTERN JAMBOREE PROGRAM

JIM EVANS, Publisher

Sled Allen's Arena—606 Texas Ave.—Saturday, May 27, 1950

BILL MYRICK and the MAYFIELD BROTHERS

EDD, SMOKY and HERB MAYFIELD standing, BILL MYRICK center

A *Western Jamboree* flyer features Bill Myrick and the Mayfield Brothers, the stars of a live broadcast on KSEL radio organized by Dave Stone, station manager from 1948–1953. By 1950, the *Western Jamboree* drew weekly audiences of over a thousand. Before Elvis came to town, the younger generation of Lubbock musicians admired the accomplished musicianship and driving rhythms of Bill Monroe–inspired bluegrass music played by these local stars. (Courtesy of Cindy Martin.)

In the early 1950s, McWhorter's at 1008 Texas Avenue carried a large selection of radios to help satisfy a growing national and local listenership. In 1953, Dave Stone established KDAV as the first all-country radio station in the world and created the *Sunday Party*. This weekly radio show gave local musicians many opportunities to play their kind of country music, broadcast live for the local radio fans. (Courtesy of Southwest Collection.)

KDUB-TV, Channel 13, was established in Lubbock in 1952. Television reached Lubbock when Dub Rogers took a chance and started the first television station in West Texas. Hosted by Jack Huddle, *The Circle 13 Dude Ranch* was a KDUB live broadcast that offered Lubbock area musicians performance time with the station's band. Waylon Jennings was lead guitarist for the Dude Ranch Band. (Courtesy of Southwest Collection.)

Plaza Shopping Center draws eager shoppers in the early 1950s. After the war, Lubbock started rapidly expanding south of Nineteenth Street. The housing development of Green Acres gained a shopping center at Twenty-sixth Street and Boston Avenue, ushering in the trend of developing neighborhood shopping centers to accommodate new residential areas as the town grew to the south and west. Downtown Lubbock was gradually losing its grip on the retail market. (Courtesy of Southwest Collection.)

Thirty-fourth Street thrives in the mid-1950s. In 1950, Thirty-fourth Street was still in the country, with the Five-Point Drive-In just west of Slide Road. In the next five years, the street would develop into a vibrant commercial artery of the town from Avenue Q to Quaker, offering drive-through eateries plus a variety of convenient mom-and-pop retail stores to a growing car culture. (Courtesy of City of Lubbock.)

76

This is an aerial view of the Circle Drive-In around 1953. In Lubbock, drive-in movies were very popular throughout the 1950s. The Circle was located on the Tahoka Highway, just north of the infamous traffic circle, a roundabout south of town that became more dangerous by the decade as truck traffic increased. (Courtesy of Southwest Collection.)

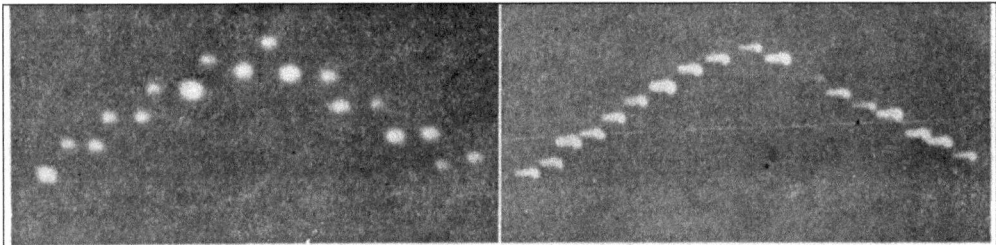

MYSTERIOUS OBJECTS IN LUBBOCK SKY—It's anybody's guess what they are, but the mysterious objects in the photos above are believed to be the "things" which Lubbockites have been seeing in the sky during recent nights. The highly unusual photos, snapped by Carl Hart, jr., of 2332 Nineteenth street, Thursday night, show what Hart said was the unidentified glowing objects as they passed over the city from north to south. In the photo at left, the dots are in a two-row V-formation, while the photo at right shows them shifted into a single-file formation. Several Lubbock residents reported seeing the objects over the city last night. Hart said he shot the two photos above with a 35mm camera.

★ ★ ★ ★ ★ ★ ★ ★ ★ ★ ★ ★ ★ ★
FOWL OR SAUCERS -- STRANGE OBJECTS REPORTED IN AREA

Flying 'Whatsits' Seen Again

By KENNETH MAY
Avalanche Staff Writer

THE "flying whatsits" continued to zoom through Lubbock skies Friday night as numerous residents reported seeing flashes of light flying at "unbelievable speeds"—and at least one person showed up photographs of what he said he saw in the sky.

Identity of the strange objects continued to baffle all who claimed to have seen them and three Texas Tech professors who ex- amined photographs taken by Carl Hart, jr., 18-year-old amateur photographer of 2332 Nineteenth street, could offer no explanation.

The objects—whatever they are—were reportedly seen over Lubbock at at least three distinct times, from 8:40 p. m. to 10:37 p. m. Friday. Morning Avalanche editorial offices received numerous calls from persons who said they had seen the light formations.

Number Of Objects Vary

All those reporting the objects described them as flying in V-shaped or U-shaped formations most directly overhead within from 3 to 7 seconds. The number of "dots" reported in the formations ranged from eight or nine to "20 or 30."

Dr. J. C. Cross, head of Tech's department of biology, examined photographs taken by Hart and said he could offer no explanation as to their identity. In answer to the theory of some that the dots may have been birds leaving a phosphorescent glow, he asserted, "It definitely wasn't caused by birds."

A Lubbock county farmer, T. E. Snider, jr., of Lubbock, Route 3, reported later in the night that "I saw something like people have been seeing and it definitely was ducks." Although not accounting for the unbelievable speed reported by others, Snider said that a reflection form the Westerner

The Lubbock Lights was a UFO sighting that has inspired book chapters and even a rock opera. On August 25, 1951, three Texas Tech professors sitting outside together observed a total of 20 to 30 lights flying overhead. On August 30, 1951, Texas Tech student Carl Hart Jr. saw the lights and took a photograph that was reprinted in newspapers and *Life* magazine. (Courtesy of Southwest Collection.)

A Lubbock County sheriff's posse in the 1951 ABC Rodeo Parade rides by the old post office. The group had no connection with the sheriff's office; it was a riding club trying to keep the spirit of the Old West alive. The ABC Rodeo was started in 1940 to support the Lubbock Boys and Girls Clubs and continues to be a top rodeo today. (Courtesy of Jerry Matthews.)

In 1955, Lubbock Lions cook pancakes for a crowd. In 1952, the Lubbock Lions Club began holding an annual pancake breakfast to help support its charitable activities. By 1960, the Lubbock chapter had become the largest in the nation, and remains so today. In 2009, the Lubbock Lions Club set the world record for serving the most pancakes in eight hours—cooking 66,549 pancakes for some 17,000 people. (Courtesy of Southwest Collection.)

Four

THE COTTONEST CITY
IN ALL THE WORLD

Throughout the 1950s and 1960s, Lubbock agribusiness grew in volume and complexity. Cotton farming was a very lucrative enterprise during these decades and became more and more mechanized. Tractors got larger and cotton strippers became more efficient. A prolonged drought throughout the 1950s, accompanied by more and more irrigated farmland, lowered the water table significantly, and the region began to implement conservation measures.

The growing mechanization of agriculture in Lubbock gradually lessened the need for seasonal workers, so many settled in to take other jobs. By the 1960s, Hispanic culture was firmly established in Lubbock, with a population of 11,000 people adding to the small business culture of the town with restaurants, bakeries, and retail shops.

These economic boom times brought new urban growth, with the old Lubbock banks constructing contemporary high-rises downtown. In 1958, the 20-story Great Plains Life Building and a new courthouse were completed. The stately stone courthouse was demolished in the 1960s.

By 1956, the musical influence of early television and radio had successfully nurtured the talents of a new generation of musicians. Deeply influenced by the Lubbock performances of Elvis Presley during 1955 and 1956, Buddy Holly and his musical compatriots Jerry Allison, Joe B. Mauldin, and Niki Sullivan broke onto the national music scene in 1957 with their hit "That'll Be the Day." Throughout 1957, the music of Buddy Holly and the Crickets topped the *Billboard* charts—only to stop with Holly's death in a 1959 plane crash that also killed Ritchie Valens and The Big Bopper. A generation wept. The event is immortalized in the song "American Pie" by Don McLean.

In 1956, Texas Technological College was finally accepted into the Southwest Conference, due in large measure to the newly constructed Lubbock Municipal Auditorium and Coliseum. Throughout the 1960s, the college continued to grow in students and stature. In 1969, with the help of longtime Lubbock politician and Texas governor Preston E. Smith, Texas Tech became part of the state university system as Texas Tech University.

Pictured in the 1950s, the Hi-D-Ho on North College Avenue (University) was a favorite gathering spot for Buddy Holly and his musician friends. Postwar teenagers were a restless lot, many identifying with the poignant confusions of movie idols Marlon Brando and James Dean. Most had cars, and the Hi-D-Ho Drive-Ins were favorite stopping places as they cruised the town day and night. (Courtesy of Southwest Collection.)

Lubbock teens enjoy an evening together dancing the bop. By 1955, Lubbock had six radio and two television stations, introducing the latest music and trends to the town. Late at night, the airwaves brought black programming from Shreveport into Lubbock. KSEL played the renegade country music of the *Louisiana Hayride*, and postwar teenagers were paying attention and responding to these new sounds. (Courtesy of Southwest Collection.)

A 1950s newspaper ad announcing a Cotton Club performance by Fats Domino was a sign of new times in Lubbock. The war broke up the big bands and dance traditions of the 1930s and 1940s, and the Cotton Club responded to new ways by sometimes booking black musicians. Tommy Hancock kept the tradition alive when he established the New Cotton Club in 1960 on the Slaton Highway. (Courtesy of Cindy Martin.)

FATS DOMINO
AND HIS ORCHESTRA
— AT THE —
COTTON
CLUB
SAT. NIGHT, JUNE 9
ADVANCE TICKETS
— ON SALE —
WAYNE'S 34TH
2237 34th
SH4-1464

Elvis Presley charms Lubbock fans. In 1954, the Fair Park Coliseum was built just in time for Dave Stone to book Elvis in January 1955. Elvis was back by popular demand five more times that year. His performances changed the way young West Texas musicians played their songs. They admired his music and his effect on young women. (Courtesy of Steve Bonner.)

BY POPULAR DEMAND

ELVIS
PRESLEY

The Be-Bop Western
Star of the LA. Hay-
ride Returns to Lub-
bock.

4:00 P.M. MATINEE
TODAY ONLY
FAIR PARK COLISEUM

ALSO ON THE BIG WESTERN SHOW:

DUKE OF PADUCAH—of the Grand Ole Opry
"Get On The Wagon, Boys, These Shoes Are
Killing Me."

CHARLENE ARTHUR—Miss Dynamite of the Big D Jamboree and Victor Records.

JIMMIE RODGERS SNOW—Son of Hank Snow and Victor Recording Artist

ACE BALL—Okeh Recording Artist

BILL MYRICK and the RAINBOW RIDERS

BUDDY AND BOB

BOXOFFICE OPENS AT 2:30

Buddy Holly and Bob Montgomery, known as Buddy and Bob, performed at this one event with Elvis, who returned to Lubbock six more times in 1956 before anyone thought he was controversial. Lubbock musicians recognized his music as a rhythm-driven country sound, similar to their own. Soon, a traditional country string band that added a strong blues-rhythm backbeat would be known as rockabilly. (Courtesy of Cindy Martin.)

Buddy Holly and Bob Montgomery play a gig at Fair Park Coliseum. Lubbock was full of serious and talented young musicians available as pickup bands for all kinds of promotional events. In 1956, Sonny Curtis and Buddy Holly cut a few country singles in Nashville for Decca, but Nashville seemed musically confining to them, and they came home disappointed. (Courtesy of Steve Bonner.)

This is a promotional photograph of Buddy Holly and the Crickets. On fall weekends in 1956, Lawson's Roller Rink became a teen live-music venue. Holly gathered musician friends Jerry Allison, Joe B. Mauldin, and Niki Sullivan to play these gigs, perfecting their Elvis-inspired rockabilly sound and cutting their first record at the Norman Petty Studio in February 1957. "That'll Be the Day" launched the group's career. (Courtesy of Steve Bonner.)

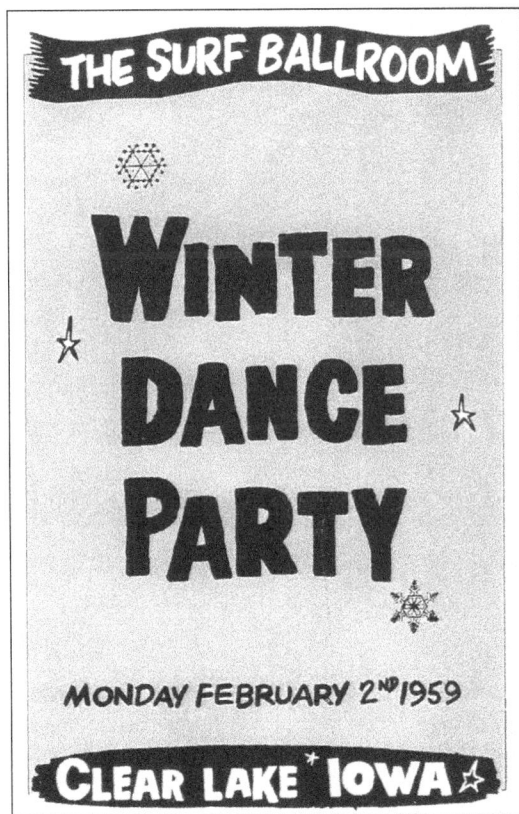

This poster advertises the fateful Winter Dance Party of 1959. Throughout 1957, music by Buddy Holly and the Crickets topped *Billboard* charts. They performed on the *Ed Sullivan Show* and even at the Apollo in Harlem. In 1958, Holly married and the band split up. Waylon Jennings and *Texas Playboys* musician Tommy Allsup joined Holly on tour until Holly was killed in a plane crash on February 3, 1959, leaving Clear Lake, Iowa. (Courtesy of Cindy Martin.)

Buddy Holly is buried at the Lubbock Cemetery. A great influence on the music to follow, Holly was a disciplined instrumentalist who wrote his own songs, setting the standard for bands to come. The combination of drums, bass, rhythm guitar, and lead guitar was also thereafter the standard. A black group called The Spiders inspired the name The Crickets, and from that name came The Beatles. (Courtesy of Visit Lubbock.)

Ralna English performs in hometown Lubbock around 1955. From 1969 to 1982, English was a regular on *The Lawrence Welk Show*. Tex Logan, a Texas Tech engineering graduate, fiddler, and folk festival favorite, joined The New Lost City Ramblers in 1959. Before Virgil Johnson became principal of Dunbar, he was a member of The Velvets, a doo-wop group with the 1961 hit "Tonight's the Night." (Courtesy of Ralna English.)

A mid-century tractor with stripper eases the cotton harvest. During the 1950s, cotton farming became more and more mechanized. Tractors became larger, and cotton strippers and rotary cutters changed the labor needs for the harvest. Lubbock began to claim it was the most mechanized farming region in the world. (Courtesy of Louise Underwood.)

Plains Cooperative Oil Mill was located at Nineteenth Street and Avenue A. By the 1950s, Plains Co-op was one of Lubbock's largest agribusinesses, producing cottonseed oil, cattle feed, and other cotton by-products. Plains Cotton Cooperative Association was established in 1952 as the marketing arm of the regional industry, and developed high-speed instrumentation to evaluate cotton quality and improve regional marketing, ultimately influencing USDA cotton-classing procedures. (Courtesy of Southwest Collection.)

This parade float celebrates the bumper cotton crop of 1947 that overwhelmed gins, warehouses, and railroads and generated $32.8 million in farm income. The postwar cotton boom lasted into the 1960s, nurturing an agribusiness complex of compresses, oil mills, and gins that represented an annual investment of over $100 million. In 1960, the chamber of commerce claimed Lubbock was the "Cottonest City in All the World." (Courtesy of Southwest Collection.)

Through cheap gas and abundant water from the Ogallala Aquifer, Lubbock farmers overcame the drought of the 1950s through irrigation, causing a widespread decline in the water table by 1956. This awareness led to concerted conservation measures to sustain regional row-crop agriculture. From irrigation technology to territorial law suits to regulatory measures, Lubbock leaders began to keep an anxious eye on water. (Courtesy of Jerod Foster.)

Roughnecks work an oil rig near Lubbock. From 1945 to 1960, the petroleum industry contributed substantially to the economy of Lubbock through active development of oil fields and petroleum industry services. After a significant decline in the late 20th century, petroleum has returned as a significant economic engine for West Texas. (Courtesy of Southwest Collection.)

The Burrus Elevators on Fourth Street added an imposing rural statement to the Lubbock landscape until demolished in 2004 to make way for the Marsha Sharp Freeway. A grain storage and feedlot industry developed in the late 1950s, with significant acreage devoted to hybrid grain sorghum, a drought-resistant feed developed at the Texas A&M Experiment Station (now the Texas A&M AgriLife Research and Extension Center) in Lubbock. (Courtesy of Southwest Collection.)

An aerial view of downtown Lubbock from around 1956 shows the urban growth of the town, with high-rises at least attempting to impose their contemporary splendor on the vast flatlands of the region. In 1950, the population of Lubbock had grown to 71,747, and by 1960 topped 128,000, with the promise of continuing growth for the foreseeable future. (Courtesy of Southwest Collection.)

This c. 1958 photograph shows the current Lubbock County Courthouse, with the old Lubbock County Courthouse still intact right behind it. The Lubbock County Commissioners Court decided to take land from Courthouse Square to build a new courthouse. The old structure was ultimately demolished, destroying the time-honored gathering place of the town and a meaningful heritage building in the course of a decade. (Courtesy of Southwest Collection.)

Construction of the new Lubbock National Bank building at Main Street and Texas Avenue was completed in 1953. Soon, the last vestiges of the war would be gone, with the Army Store demolished to make room for a drive-through. (Courtesy of Southwest Collection.)

The 20-story Great Plains Life Building (Metro Tower) was completed in 1958. Until 1967, First National Bank made the building its home. Radio station KLLL also broadcast from the building, offering listeners an all-country format and commentary from deejays Waylon Jennings and owner Sky Corbin. Some say the radio announcer in Greater Tuna is modeled on Sky Corbin. Today, this is still the tallest building in town. (Courtesy of Southwest Collection.)

Supporters attend the 1957 opening ceremony for Lubbock Christian College, a private educational institution supported by members of the Church of Christ. From a junior college in 1957, the school became a fully accredited four-year college in 1972 and a full-fledged university in 1988. Located at 5601 Nineteenth Street, Lubbock Christian represented the westward movement of the town at its opening. (Courtesy of Lubbock Christian University.)

Lubbock's second television station, KCBD, was established in 1953 as a primary NBC affiliate. In 1969, KSEL, now KAMC, became the primary and exclusive ABC affiliate for the Lubbock market. KDUB, the first television station in the nation to serve a medium-sized market, remains the CBS affiliate today, as KLBK. (Courtesy of Southwest Collection.)

This Mexican bakery served the growing Hispanic community of Lubbock in the 1960s. By 1960, Hispanic culture was firmly established in Lubbock and building a significant commercial presence. Jose S. Ramirez owned a popular Mexican restaurant at Fiftieth Street and Avenue H (I-27) and became the first Hispanic school board member in 1974. (Courtesy of Southwest Collection.)

La Feria, located at Broadway and Avenue G, offered Hispanics a festive gathering spot to browse, buy, and socialize on the east edge of downtown. (Courtesy of Elda Moreno.)

This is a 1950s view of the original St. Joseph's Catholic Church built in 1924. The Guadalupe neighborhood grew up around the church, and in 1963, the parish built the stately brick structure that still serves the congregation today. (Courtesy of St. Joseph's Catholic Church.)

Children gather for a school picture outside the new Guadalupe Elementary, built in 1961. In 1951, nearly 60,000 seasonal workers were employed in Lubbock and Crosby Counties at cotton harvest time. By 1960, the number was 18,000. The Lubbock Hispanic community was firmly settled and growing, with a population of 11,642 in the 1950 US Census. (Courtesy of Southwest Collection.)

Students attend a school assembly in the early 1950s at the Lubbock High School auditorium. Until 1956, this lovely auditorium served as the largest formal gathering place in Lubbock, hosting many dignitaries through the years, including Eleanor Roosevelt and Lyndon B. Johnson. (Courtesy of Southwest Collection.)

As Tech, Lubbock Welcomed Entry Into SWC—In Pictures!

In The Huddle At Last!

SOUTHWEST CONFERENCE

EXTRA!
TOREADOR
FINALLY!
TECH MAKES SWC

A jubilant media responds to Texas Tech finally being accepted into the Southwest Conference in 1956. Lubbock and Texas Tech had been trying to gain entry for years, and in deep frustration, many Lubbock families canceled their Neiman-Marcus credit cards in a 1952 protest, convinced Southern Methodist University, located in the store's home city of Dallas, was the roadblock to Texas Tech becoming a part of the conference. (Courtesy of Southwest Collection.)

Lubbock Municipal Auditorium and Coliseum was completed in 1956 through a joint venture between the City of Lubbock and Texas Technological College. The 10,000-seat coliseum was built primarily for Texas Tech basketball games and played a significant role in the school entering the Southwest Conference. (Courtesy of Southwest Collection.)

This aerial view shows the proximity of the Municipal Auditorium and Coliseum to Jones Stadium during a Southwest Conference football game, played to a packed crowd in 1961. Originally built in 1947 with a donation from outgoing Texas Tech president Clifford B. Jones, Jones Stadium was renovated in 1961, adding a recessed field and seating capacity for 41,000. (Courtesy of Southwest Collection.)

The statue of Will Rogers was created by Electra Waggoner Biggs and presented to Texas Tech by the Amon G. Carter Foundation in 1950. The statue remains a fond symbol of school pride. By 1962, Texas Tech had an enrollment of 10,428 and continually vied for the place of second-largest institution of higher learning in Texas. In 1964, the board of directors voted to make the college a university. (Courtesy of Southwest Collection.)

Texas Tech students protest for their views in the name-change controversy. Alums wanted to keep the double-T logo and the name they loved. Students, rather heatedly, argued for the name Texas State University, but the alums won. In 1969, Texas Technological College joined the state university system with an official nickname, Texas Tech University. (Courtesy of Southwest Collection.)

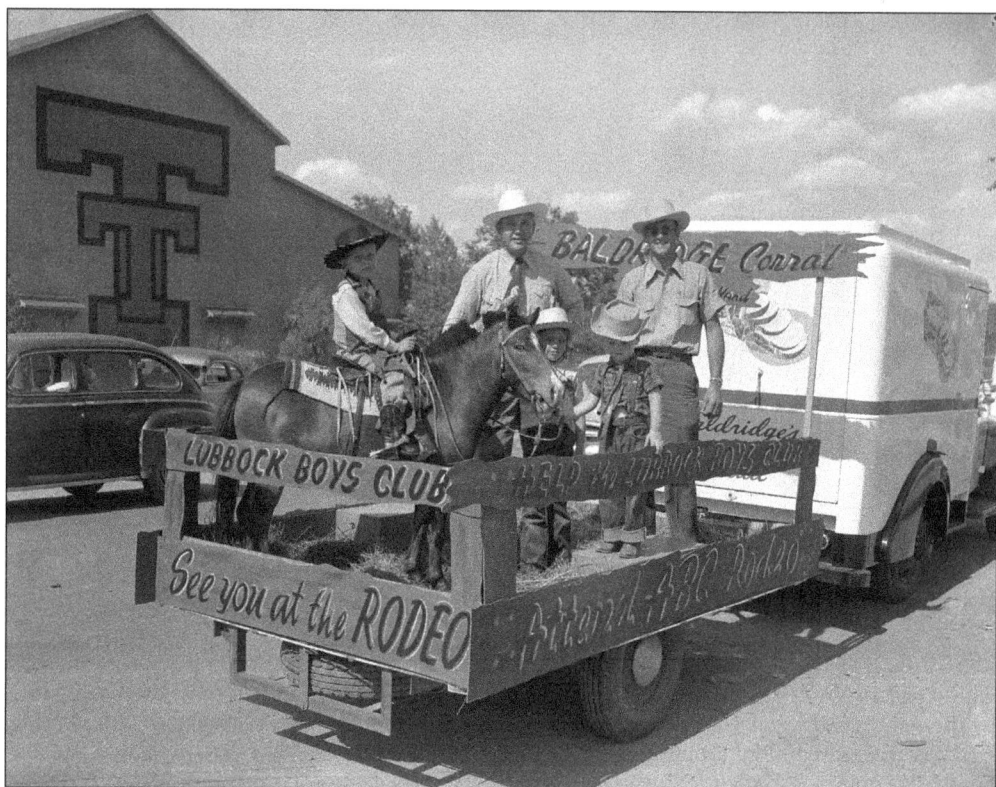

A 1950s rodeo float marks the end of the parade trail across from the old Texas Tech men's gym. Lubbock continues to celebrate its western heritage through the ABC Rodeo and the Texas Tech Rodeo and Rodeo Club. In 1955, the Texas Tech team won the championship at the College National Finals Rodeo and continues to win regional and national championships today. (Courtesy of Southwest Collection.)

The Goin' Band from Raiderland is in classic field formation under the direction of Dean Killion, who served as director of bands from 1959 to 1981. The band got its name by being the first to travel to games out of town. So taken with the novelty of a band traveling to out-of-town games, Will Rogers financed one of the band's trips to Fort Worth in the late 1930s. (Courtesy of Southwest Collection.)

The composition of the 1959 Farm-Pac Employee Baseball League champions indicates the racial changes that were occurring in Lubbock. In 1955, Lubbock integrated all of its elementary schools without incident. Secondary schools would take much longer, but the deep racial lines traditionally drawn by the town were beginning to crumble. (Courtesy of City of Lubbock.)

Summer bathers enjoy the Mackenzie Park swimming pool in 1955, the year Hispanics were officially granted permission to swim in the municipal pools at Clapp Park and Mackenzie. That same year, the City of Lubbock created the Department of Parks and Recreation to manage the 31 parks the city had already developed, and in 1960, opened the Garden and Arts Center at Clapp Park. (Courtesy of Southwest Collection.)

This aerial view of Monterey Shopping Center around 1960 shows an easily accessible parking lot full of cars, with the very contemporary entrance to the new Hemphill-Wells in the foreground. In 1955, Monterey High School opened at Forty-ninth Street and Indiana Avenue. That same year, Caprock Shopping Center and Monterey Shopping Center opened at Elgin Avenue on Fiftieth Street, leading Lubbock shoppers farther and farther away from downtown. (Courtesy of Southwest Collection.)

Hordes of shoppers gather outside the new Woolworth's at Monterey Shopping Center in the late 1950s. Caprock Shopping Center offered similar shopping and parking amenities, just across Elgin to the east. Dunlap's Department Store built its flagship store at Caprock, establishing Lubbock as company headquarters and remaining there until the 1990s. A Furr's Cafeteria was also available at Caprock through the 1990s. (Courtesy of Southwest Collection.)

This is a Dunbar High School basketball game in the 1950s, when the Dunbar Panthers excelled against other black teams in the state. By the mid-1960s, Lubbock high schools were integrated. Coronado High School was built in 1965 to respond to city growth west of town. Estacado High School was built in 1967 to serve students in northeast Lubbock. Dunbar later became a junior high school. (Courtesy of Southwest Collection.)

In this iconic view, the Strip is bedecked in neon, like a mini-Vegas located in a cotton field. In 1960, the town of Slaton in Lubbock County District 2 voted to sell liquor and inspired a curiosity called the Strip—a line of liquor stores on the Tahoka Highway right outside the Lubbock city limits. Stores offered carryout service, and customers often made selections without leaving their car. (Courtesy of Cindy Martin.)

Lubbock Army Air Field was reactivated as Reese Air Force Base in 1949. Reese proved to be a consistent economic engine for Lubbock, at one time employing as many as 650 civilian workers and 2,800 airmen. The facility became a jet-training base in 1959 and played a significant role in the Vietnam War, with off-base housing supporting as many as 2,500 people involved in the conflict. (Courtesy of Southwest Collection.)

This family shows its anxiety at sending a beloved young man off to war in the late 1960s. Primarily, the Vietnam War was fought by young men from poor and immigrant families who had no thought nor means of pursuing a higher education. Lubbock remained a very loyal and patriotic city, as did Texas Tech, where no significant student protests occurred. (Courtesy of Southwest Collection.)

Five

"UNBELIEVABLE!"

The F5 tornado that hit the heart of Lubbock on May 11, 1970, was an unbelievable occurrence for the town: killing 26 people, wounding 1,100, and causing $40 million in damages. To this day, the tornado haunts people's imaginations—inspiring songs, festivals, and art exhibitions that address mortality while celebrating resilience.

Support from the state and federal governments, coupled with a $13.6 million local bond issue, gave Lubbock the opportunity to embark on an urban renewal project, resulting in a multipurpose convention center, a contemporary public library, and a recreational lake system. Disaster relief funds also helped rebuild Guadalupe into a stable and charming neighborhood.

In 1972, the South Plains Mall opened on the far south and west side of town, virtually ending retail trade downtown and nurturing residential development south beyond the Loop—a highway finished in 1970 around the perimeter of the city. By 1980, Lubbock was developing on Eighty-second Street, and on Ninety-eighth Street by 1990. By 2013, there was residential development south to 130th Street (FM 1585) and west of Milwaukee Avenue.

While the tornado and the mall changed the configuration of the town, the very nature of the times also affected Lubbock. Throughout the 1970s and 1980s, Lubbock was an exciting party town, full of local and regional live music acts. The era also brought about significant political activism, with women, blacks, and Hispanics loudly insisting on meaningful representation—and they finally got it.

Today, Lubbock is a vibrant center for the arts, as well as a significant tertiary medical care center and a sports destination for the region. Texas Tech has grown into a system that includes San Angelo State University and the El Paso Medical School. In 2006, Kings Dominion became the first residential development on the Eastside in 50 years. Hispanics now represent 38 percent of the population and contribute significantly to the city's small business and professional world. So much change in just one century is sometimes unbelievable.

This is an aerial view of devastation after the Lubbock Tornado. At 9:46 p.m. on May 11, 1970, Lubbock sustained a direct hit from a massive F5 tornado, slashing a path 1.5 miles wide and 8 miles long through downtown Lubbock, the Guadalupe neighborhood, and the Lubbock Country Club area. It proceeded in the wake of a huge hailstorm, and no one saw it coming. People just kept saying "unbelievable." (Courtesy of City of Lubbock.)

Family members in the Guadalupe neighborhood search, and hope, for something to salvage. Located just north of downtown, Guadalupe was turned to rubble as houses collapsed on inhabitants. Many were left homeless and given temporary quarters in federally owned housing, with members of the Lubbock Bar Association volunteering assistance with property insurance and other legal issues. (Courtesy of Rodney Goebel.)

Residents confront the damage to their house on Main Street near Avenue L. The First National Bank-Pioneer Gas Building (Wells Fargo) shows its wounds in the background. This "glass box" International Style building sustained over $1 million in damages. With winds up to 200 mph, the tornado wrecked 500 businesses, damaged 10,000 houses, and totally destroyed 1,100 homes, leaving 1,800 people homeless. (Courtesy of Rodney Goebel.)

This fire truck managed to survive the collapse of the downtown firehouse, but most vehicles were not so lucky. Over 10,000 vehicles were damaged by the storm, and 25,000 telephones lost service, some for days on end. Miraculously, the emergency radio station, KFYO, maintained an open phone line and was the only consistent communications link to the outside world right after the storm. (Courtesy of City of Lubbock.)

Cumberland Presbyterian Church became the iconic symbol of the devastation brought on by the Lubbock Tornado. Located at 901 Avenue O, the newly built church was leveled. During the eight-minute rampage, 26 people died, 1,100 were wounded, and $40 million in property losses were caused by the tornado. (Courtesy of Karen Martin.)

A makeshift emergency shelter in the Coliseum offered medical care, food, and clothing to people displaced by the tornado. Within two hours of the storm, Mayor James H. Granberry, City Manager Bill Blackwell, and William A. Payne had implemented emergency operations. On May 13, Pres. Richard M. Nixon declared Lubbock a disaster area, and the National Guard was called in to control looting. (Courtesy of City of Lubbock.)

This aerial view shows the new entertainment and convention center, plus a new library, built out of the ruins on Sixth Street (Mac Davis Lane) off Avenue Q. In August 1970, Lubbock voted in a recovery bond of $13.6 million to supplement $37 million in state and federal disaster relief, and the city embarked on a massive downtown urban renewal project. (Courtesy of Southwest Collection.)

The George and Helen Mahon Library opened in 1974. Today, Mahon serves as the main branch of a four-branch public library system. It was only in 1954 that Lubbock built its first stand-alone library, thanks in large part to the tireless efforts of Daisy Godeke and the Lubbock Women's Club. Before that, the library was shuffled from one room to another at the courthouse. (Courtesy of City of Lubbock.)

The Lubbock Memorial Civic Center opened in 1977 as a multipurpose events center and was dedicated to the memory of the 26 people who died in the tornado. The 1,377-seat theater became the home of the Lubbock Symphony Orchestra and the young and growing Ballet Lubbock. Designed to accommodate gatherings of every configuration, the civic center gave Lubbock the opportunity to become a regional hub for festivals and conventions. (Courtesy of City of Lubbock.)

Travelers wait in line at Southwest Airlines in the Lubbock airport. Just before the tornado, Lubbock voters approved a $14 million bond package to build a modern airport that opened in 1976 with seven gates. Southwest Airlines came to Lubbock in 1978, offering inexpensive flights throughout the region. Today, Lubbock Preston Smith International Airport has 10 gates and is also served by American Airlines and United Airlines. (Courtesy of City of Lubbock.)

The South Plains Mall opened in 1972. The mall dramatically changed Lubbock by bringing hundreds of new vendors to town and changing traditional shopping patterns. From 1960 to 1970, the city constructed a circular highway around the outer perimeter of the town, and the mall was built at Slide Road and Loop 289, drawing businesses away from downtown. (Courtesy of City of Lubbock.)

In 1970, St. Mary of the Plains Hospital opened a new contemporary facility between Memphis and Quaker Avenues on Twenty-fourth Street, just west of Methodist Hospital. Over the years, the area around the two facilities has developed into a strong and diverse medical district, serving the whole region in every area of need. In 1998, St. Mary's and Methodist merged to become Covenant Health System. (Courtesy of Covenant.)

The Texas Tech University School of Medicine opened in 1972. As governor of Texas from 1969 to 1973, Preston A. Smith established the School of Medicine. A teaching hospital, Lubbock General Hospital (University Medical Center), was added in 1978, and with the addition of the School of Nursing and School of Allied Health, this medical teaching institution became the Texas Tech University Health Sciences Center. (Courtesy of Southwest Collection.)

The Museum of Texas Tech University moved into this contemporary facility at Fourth Street and Indiana Avenue in 1970. Today, the museum holds over five million objects, many on temporary or permanent display to the general public. The Museum on Fourth Street and the School of Law, opening in 1967 on Nineteenth Street and Hartford, framed the western expansion of the campus in 1970. (Courtesy of Cindy Martin.)

Located just east of the museum, the Ranching Heritage Center opened in 1976 as a rich celebration of ranch history, featuring authentic buildings from the 18th century through the mid-20th century and self-guided tours to experience ranch culture. Dr. Curry Holden established the center and used rubble from the Lubbock tornado in his landscaping scheme. (Courtesy of Cindy Martin.)

The 1976 football season added to the spirit of well-being about the general recovery of the city. Coach Steve Sloan led the Red Raiders to eight straight wins, with the sweetest being the October 30 home game when Texas Tech beat the University of Texas 31-28. (Courtesy of Southwest Collection.)

Stubb's Bar-B-Q was established in 1968 on East Broadway. Throughout the 1970s, Stubb's was a vital part of the dynamic Lubbock music scene, where a new generation of local musicians was experimenting with its own brand of country-rock. Christopher B. "Stubb" Stubblefield brought blues artists like B.B. King to Lubbock and nurtured new talent through his Sunday Night Jams, when anyone could take the mike. (Courtesy of Cindy Martin.)

The Flatlanders, Joe Ely, Jimmie Dale Gilmore, and Butch Hancock, perform with Steve Wesson on autoharp and Tony Pearson on mandolin. The band existed from 1972 to 1973. In 1991, band sessions with Rounder Records were released as *More a Legend Than a Band*, bringing new acclaim and old friends and songwriters Ely, Gilmore, and Hancock back together to perform as The Flatlanders. (Courtesy of Southwest Collection.)

110

The Supernatural Family Band was comprised of Tommy Hancock, his wife, Charlene, their son and daughters, cousins, and anyone else who wanted to join them in fun or high seriousness. The new Cotton Club was a significant live music and dance venue through the 1970s, with Hancock improvising at every turn and giving a new generation of Lubbock musicians a place to experiment and feel at home. (Courtesy of Southwest Collection.)

The Cobras perform at Fat Dawg's in the early 1980s. In 1972, Lubbock voted in liquor-by-the-drink, and bars blossomed all over the place. In 1978, Fat Dawg's began booking R&B groups from downstate—blues artists like Stevie Ray Vaughan and performance acts like Los Lobos, plus talented locals like Joe Ely, instigating a small-club live music scene in Lubbock. (Courtesy of Southwest Collection.)

The Joe Ely Band was organized in 1977 and showcased the talents of many Lubbock musicians, including Jesse "Guitar" Taylor on electric guitar, Lloyd Maines on steel guitar, and Ponte Bone on accordion. The band recorded and toured to great success, with a sweep through Europe opening for The Clash and performances with Linda Ronstadt and the Rolling Stones. (Courtesy of Southwest Collection.)

Organized in 1977, The Maines Brothers Band became a popular country-rock band and helped carry on the tradition of West Texas family music-making. The uncles and father of the four Maines brothers in the group performed as a regional band in the 1950s. Solo artist Natalie Maines was lead singer for the Dixie Chicks and represents the third generation of talented performers from this musical family. (Courtesy of Robert Hudnall.)

Terry Allen poses in his studio with a cast of Stubb's statue, a bronze exhibited at the Stubb's Bar-B-Q site on East Broadway. Son of early Lubbock sports promoter Sled Allen, Terry is also an unofficial band member of The Flatlanders. He is a celebrated sculptor and musical performer, as well as a songwriter, penning popular "Amarillo Highway" and memorial song "Lubbock Tornado," now a popular ringtone. (Courtesy of Terry Allen.)

Joe Ely, Linda Ronstadt, and Jesse Taylor take center stage at the 1982 Tornado Jam in Buddy Holly Park, a commemoration of the Lubbock Tornado organized by Joe Ely in 1980. A crowd of 8,000 came the first year, 30,000 the next, and 50,000 in 1982. City leaders found the festival disquieting and outlawed it, claiming the crowds were harming the buffalo grass. (Courtesy of Bill Boon.)

Aztlan Park was built after the tornado in Guadalupe. US Small Business Administration and disaster relief funding helped people rebuild Guadalupe, with the park added as part of this revitalization project. The park site was one of the largest migrant worker camps in Lubbock. This Emmanuel Martinez mural and a Texas historical marker help commemorate the Hispanic history of the town. (Courtesy of City of Lubbock.)

Ernesto Barton hosts his KLBK weekly television program *Si Se Puede*. In 1977, Bidal Aguero established the bilingual weekly newspaper *El Editor*, reaching out to a growing and politically active Hispanic community dispersed to new areas of town after the tornado. In 1979, Barton started another weekly, the *West Texas Hispanic News*, established his television program, and in the 1990s, founded a Hispanic radio station. (Courtesy of *Avalanche Journal*.)

Conrado Cavazos serves up savory Mexican fare at Lala's Restaurant at 1110 Broadway. Conrado and wife, Lala, opened their popular eatery in 1981, and it quickly became an important venue for political gatherings, as well as good food. In 1984, after years of court wrangling, Lubbock adopted single-member districts, giving Lubbock minority populations neighborhood-based representation on the Lubbock City Council. (Courtesy of Southwest Collection.)

KCBD-TV news anchors Karen McCay and Abner Euresti reflect the new diversity of Lubbock in 1983. In 1970, Joan Ervin became the first African American on the Lubbock school board. In 1974, Carolyn Jordan became the first woman on the Lubbock City Council. In 1984, Maggie Trejo and T.J. Patterson joined the Lubbock City Council, and in 1985, Eliseo Solis became Lubbock County commissioner. (Courtesy of Southwest Collection.)

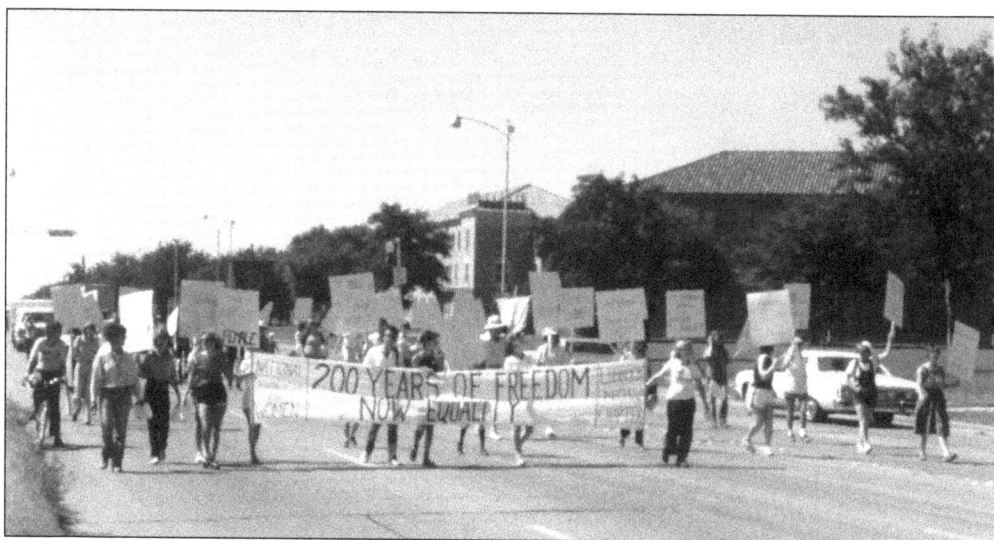

Lubbock women march in support of the Equal Rights Amendment in 1976. The feminist movement and the ERA gained support through the Lubbock chapter of the National Organization for Women. Lubbock NOW also gave voice to the issue of violence against women and helped organize a battered women's shelter. Women's Protective Services was established in 1979 with support from the Junior League. (Courtesy of Southwest Collection.)

Eddie Richardson, his mother, and T.J. Patterson receive a 25-year award for their weekly newspaper, *Southwest Digest*, started in 1977 and serving the South Plains today. The black community also shows its hegemony through the Federation of Choirs. Each spring the Federation of Choirs puts on a rousing and glorious gospel performance, with choir members from 11 Eastside churches. (Courtesy of T.J. Patterson.)

The Lubbock Arts Festival is held each spring at the Lubbock Memorial Civic Center. Sponsored by the Lubbock Arts Alliance, the event offers the general public a celebratory weekend of all things artistic. Each year, the civic center facility also plays host to the National Cowboy Symposium, a weekend celebration of cowboy culture from poetry to food. (Courtesy of the Lubbock Arts Alliance.)

Dancers perform at Fiestas del Llano, the annual celebration of Mexican independence. Starting with the crowning of an annual Miss Hispanic Lubbock and a parade down Broadway, Fiestas del Llano then turns the Lubbock Memorial Civic Center into a cultural event site full of music, dance, and savory edibles for the pleasure of the general public. (Courtesy of Cindy Martin.)

The Lubbock Christian University Chaparral baseball team won the NAIA World Series in 1983. The Chaparrals won again in 2009. The Lubbock Christian Lady Chaparral basketball team won the NAIA championship in 2006 and made the Final Four in 2012, and the Lady Chaparral softball team won the national championship in 2008, the year the program was established. (Courtesy of LCU.)

The Texas Tech Red Raiders, 1984–1985 Southwest Conference basketball champions, were led to victory by coach Gerald Myers. Sports have always been an elemental pastime in Lubbock, with Texas Tech athletics occupying a special place of attention and enthusiasm for alumni and townsfolk alike. After Gerald Myers, Bob Knight coached the Red Raiders to four Big 12 Conference championships and three co-championships between 2001 and 2008. (Courtesy of Southwest Collection.)

In 1993, Texas Tech basketball coach Marsha Sharp and the Lady Raiders captivated the nation with their civilized and improbable NCAA championship win. The spectacular performance of the Lady Raiders brought national attention to Texas Tech and sent local fans into the streets to celebrate the glorious finale of this exciting season of Lady Raider basketball. (Courtesy of Southwest Collection.)

In 1994, the Red Raiders were Southwest Conference co-champions, and coach Spike Dykes led the team to a Copper Bowl win the next year over Air Force. In 1996, the Southwest Conference dissolved and Texas Tech joined the Big 12. Mike Leach was Texas Tech football coach from 2000 to 2009, leading the team through an especially memorable 2008 season with 11 regular season wins. (Courtesy of Southwest Collection.)

Llano Estacado Winery was established in 1976 by Texas Tech professors Clinton "Doc" McPherson and Robert R. Reed. By 1986, the winery was winning wine competitions. Today, West Texas has significant grapevine acreage, and Lubbock winemakers continue to produce competitive varietals, including Doc's son Kim, owner and winemaker of McPherson Cellars, located in the historic Coca-Cola Building in the Depot District. (Courtesy of Southwest Collection.)

Anderson's Jewelry and Malouf's are now located at Kingsgate Shopping Center at Eighty-second Street and Quaker Avenue. By 1980, Lubbock had grown south of Loop 289, with the Lakeridge Country Club and residential area developing at Eighty-second Street and Vicksburg Avenue. Kingsgate Shopping Center soon followed, drawing established retailers to these new surroundings. Today, Eighty-second Street is a centrally located, bustling east-west artery to the town. (Courtesy of City of Lubbock.)

The United Spirit Arena opened on the Texas Tech campus in 1999 as home court for the Lady Raiders and Red Raider basketball teams. United Spirit Arena is named after United Supermarkets. With headquarters in Lubbock, United was family-managed for four generations and ultimately included 51 stores in 30 Texas cities. (Courtesy of Visit Lubbock.)

The Texas Tech University Education, English, and Philosophy Building, constructed in 2002, was the first academic facility built on campus since 1976. In 1996, John T. Montford became the first chancellor of the Texas Tech University system and initiated a development drive that generated $500 million in funds to be used for new buildings, scholarships, and endowed professorships. (Courtesy of Southwest Collection.)

The Depot Entertainment District on Buddy Holly Avenue (Avenue H) is the center of nightlife in Lubbock. Development of the district, ongoing since 1996, holds great promise for the revitalization of historic downtown Lubbock. Located north of Nineteenth Street downtown, the district is full of live music venues and restaurants for an evening of entertainment. It is also the heart of Lubbock's growing art scene. (Courtesy of Visit Lubbock.)

Cactus Theater musicians perform at Nostalgia Night. Saxophone player and music producer Don Caldwell owns and manages the Cactus, located on Buddy Holly Avenue. He keeps music alive in Lubbock with an ever-changing lineup, featuring his own band and famous musicians from out of town. Caldwell renovated the historic 1935 Cactus Theater to create his new venue and help develop the Depot District. (Courtesy of Don Caldwell.)

The Buddy Holly Center is located in the restored 1918 Fort Worth and Denver Depot at Nineteenth Street and Crickets Avenue (Avenue G). The center was established in 1999 to house an exhibit of Buddy Holly memorabilia and tribute to his music. It also provides Lubbock with an archival fine arts gallery for contemporary art exhibitions and courtyard summer music events. (Courtesy of Buddy Holly Center.)

The award-winning contemporary facilities of the Louise Hopkins Underwood Center for the Arts (LHUCA) are located off Fourth Street and Avenue K. Established in 2000, LHUCA serves as a dynamic incubator for Lubbock visual and performing artists. Besides offering ever-changing art exhibits and theater performances, LHUCA coordinates the First Friday Art Trail, with trolley services to art studios throughout the downtown area. (Courtesy of LHUCA.)

This is a scene from the 4th on Broadway festival, the largest annual community event in Lubbock. Starting with a long and diverse parade down Broadway, this daylong Fourth of July celebration is full of music performances, a vast food selection, and a fireworks finale in Mackenzie Park. Established in 1991, 4th on Broadway has become one of the best downtown festivals in Texas. (Courtesy of Don Caldwell.)

The American Wind Power Museum was established in 1998 across from Mackenzie Park. The museum is home to a vast collection of windmills displayed for the education and enjoyment of the general public. In 2001, the American Museum of Agriculture was established just north of Mackenzie Park and provides the general public with another opportunity to learn about Lubbock's historic rural past. (Courtesy of Visit Lubbock.)

Mac Davis stands at the Lubbock street named in his honor. Davis graduated from Lubbock High School in 1958 and after writing Elvis Presley's 1969 hit "In the Ghetto," he soon became a successful solo artist, actor, and night-show guest, as well as a prolific songwriter. From 1974 to 1976, he hosted *The Mac Davis Show* on NBC, and in 2007, a section of downtown Sixth Street in Lubbock was renamed Mac Davis Lane. (Courtesy of *Avalanche Journal*.)

Lubbock native Glenna Maxey Goodacre poses in her studio. An accomplished bronze sculptor, her works are on display throughout the nation, most notably the Vietnam Women's Memorial in Washington, DC. Lubbock's Maxey Park is named after her grandfather, and a section of Eighth Street is now named after her. (Courtesy of Cindy Martin.)

Market Street at Ninety-eighth Street and Quaker Avenue offers shoppers an abundance of take-home cuisine and gourmet foods. This store opened in 2006 to serve a growing area of town, adding a full selection of wine and beer in 2009. In that year, Lubbock voted by 64.5 percent to sell packaged alcohol inside the city limits. (Courtesy of United Supermarkets.)

This 2012 aerial view shows the Overton Project, a privately-funded, 325-acre urban renewal project undertaken by the McDougal Companies in 1999. By the 1990s, the historic North Overton Addition was in deep disrepair. Owner occupancy had dwindled to three percent and crime was rampant. Today, the neighborhood has a hotel and shopping center, boutiques, apartments to rent, and homes to buy, giving historic Lubbock new promise. (Courtesy of Visit Lubbock.)

Visitors tour the Lubbock Lake Landmark, the site of La Punta de Agua now designated a National Historic and State Archeological Landmark for the significance of the discoveries being unearthed here. The Lake Site records evidence of Singer's Store, Army camps, Spanish traders, and visits to the water by ancient peoples and animals in every North American archeological period back almost 12,000 years. (Courtesy of Visit Lubbock.)

Emcee Mac Davis leads the musical finale of the 2009 Lubbock Centennial Closing Ceremonies, with a United Spirit Arena stage full of Lubbock's finest musical talents, singing their hearts out. Lubbock celebrated its 100th birthday with a year of festivities, including an official history, dances, concerts, and memorabilia. It was a jubilant look back at humble beginnings and proud achievements during Lubbock's first century. (Courtesy of L. Scott Mann.)

Visit us at
arcadiapublishing.com

www.ingramcontent.com/pod-product-compliance
Lightning Source LLC
Chambersburg PA
CBHW050651110426

42813CB00007B/1977